BIBLICAL PRAYERS

BIBLICAL PRAYERS

Second Edition

by

LUCIEN DEISS, C.S.Sp.

7616

WORLD LIBRARY PUBLICATIONS
5040 North Ravenswood • Chicago, Illinois 60640

NIHIL OBSTAT

Lawrence J. Mick
Censor Deputatus

IMPRIMATUR

Daniel E. Pilarczyk, V.G.
Auxiliary Bishop of Cincinnati

May 26, 1976

English translation from the French was made under the direction of Fr. Alcuin L. Mikulanis, O.F.M. The First Edition of *Biblical Prayers* was edited by Fr. Paschal Varnskuhler, O.F.M., the Second Edition by Nancy Simons. Gloria Weyman was coordinator for Lucien Deiss in the United States.

First published as *Prières Bibliques,* Editions du Levain, Paris, 1974.

ISBN: 0-937690-08-2

Library of Congress Catalog Card Number: 81-51460

Printed and bound in the United States of America.

First Edition:
  First Printing — July, 1976
  Second Printing — October, 1976

Second Edition:
  First Printing — May, 1981

CONTENTS

This is not a book for "reading," but for "praying." So often we find it difficult to say the name of God and to praise his love! These prayers are meant to help. You will carry the essential burden and, at the same time, experience the most profound joy in using these formulas — they are only crutches! — to walk toward God and to encounter his love.

These prayers have their roots in Scripture. Other formulas, more up-to-date, may be desirable, even necessary. For my part, I have labored too long in the field of Scripture to wish to reap elsewhere with such abundance; I have walked too long in the forest of Tradition to be able to forget the splendors that I have encountered there.

It is precisely the experience of the timeliness of the Word for all ages, of its harmonious adaptability to our wonderful world of today — the most beautiful because it is our own and the only one in which God speaks to us — that I would like to share with you.

Lucien Deiss, C.S.Sp.
December 8

On the Feast of Our Lady,
"Servant of the Word"

INTRODUCTION

This book is intended to serve both individual prayer and community liturgical prayer. It offers prayers in the form of a litany, final orations or collects, and doxologies and blessings. The following notes deal principally with communal prayer.

LITANIES

Introduction

The litany begins with a word of introduction that takes into account the liturgical season (occasionally the feast which is being celebrated) and the nature of the prayer that follows (praise, petition, etc.).

The response is printed at the beginning of each litany. It is to be repeated after each intention, even when it is not found printed in the text.

For the community to express itself with true unity, it is preferable that the response be sung. Melodies for all the responses can be found toward the end of the book, on pages 188-193, in alphabetical order.

Intentions

Some litanies propose a large number of intentions. The assembly can thus choose those that are best suited to its prayer.

Particular intentions

At the end of the litany, members of the community who wish may offer particular intentions. These personal intentions should keep a catholic, that is, universal dimension. To cite an example, if we wish to pray for a sick person, we would freely formulate the intention in the following manner: "For all those who suffer, in particular for *N.*, who is sick, let us pray to the Lord."

Silent prayer

It is appropriate after the last personal intention to have a period of silence during which we can speak more personally with the Lord, offering him our hearts.

FINAL ORATIONS

These prayers are said by the person who presides over the celebration. In some cases, the formulas presented are rather long. They can be shortened by omitting one or another part. The essential point is not to say everything, but to pray better.

It is normal to include the Lord's Prayer, the Our Father, in a celebration. It can be placed before the final prayer. The best order seems to be the following:

— *Litanic Prayer*
  General intentions
  Particular intentions
  Silent prayer
— Our Father
— Final Oration
— Final Blessing

BLESSINGS AND DOXOLOGIES

The liturgy prefers to conclude celebrations with the blessing, "May almighty God bless you, the Father, and the Son, and the Holy Spirit." These blessings of the assembly by God may be introduced by the assembly's blessing of God, i.e., by its giving praise and thanksgiving to God who blesses his people.

What is the purpose of these blessings in liturgical celebration?

The highest form of prayer is the doxology that praises the glory of God and the blessing that returns thanks to him. It is in our praise to God that we realize ourselves most fully, inasmuch as we become the living "praise of glory" (Ephesians 1:6, 12), a calling we have received for all eternity.

This praise is found then at the heart of Christian prayer. It leads the community to that form of prayer that Jesus used in the song of jubilation (Matthew 11:25; see p. 102), the most complete expression of his faith in the Father: "I bless you, Father, Lord of heaven and of earth!"

The Spirit of Jesus has inspired all the formulas of praise that are offered here. It is also he who will create the praise in our prayer and will raise up in us a jubilant spirit.

The prayers are classified according to the seasons of the liturgical year: Advent, Christmas and Epiphany, Lent and Passiontide, the Paschal Cycle, Pentecost and the Church, feasts of Our Lady, and finally the largest section, "Prayers for All Seasons."

The boundaries of the seasons are flexible. Thus, an Advent or Lenten prayer may be used anytime during the year. It is for this reason that, at the bottom of some pages, there are notes offering suggestions for alternative uses.

ADVENT

LET THE DAY COME, LORD

Come, Lord Jesus, come!

Let the day come, Lord,
　　when our misery
will find your mercy.

Let the day come, Lord,
　　when our poverty
will find your riches.

Let the day come, Lord,
　　when our path
will find the way to your house.

Let the day come, Lord,
　　when our tears
will find your smile.

Let the day come, Lord,
　　when our joy
will find your heaven.

Let the day come, Lord,
　　when your Church
will find the Kingdom.

May you be blest, Father,
　　for that day
when our eyes will find your face!
　　Throughout all the time of our life
you have not ceased to come before us
　　in your Son Jesus Christ,
our Savior and our brother.

Let the Day Come, Lord, *Revelation 21:1-4; 22:20.*
O Wisdom (p. 3), *Sirach 24:1-22　Isaiah 9:1　Ezekiel 34:23*
Matthew 1:23　John 10　Ephesians 2:14,20　Revelation 3:7.

O WISDOM

Come, O Lord, come, save your people!

O Wisdom,
issuing from the mouth of the Most High,
announced by the prophets:
Come to teach us the way of salvation,
  Come, O Lord, come, save your people!

O Lord,
shepherd of the house of Israel,
who guide your people:
Come to redeem us by the strength of your arm,
  Come, O Lord, come, save your people!

O Son of David,
standard of people and of kings,
you whom the world implores:
Come to deliver us, Lord, do not delay,
  Come, O Lord, come, save your people!

O Key of David,
and scepter of the house of Israel,
you who open so no one can close,
you who close so no one can open:
Come to free those who wait in the darkness,
  Come, O Lord, come, save your people!

O Rising Sun,
splendor of eternal light and sun of justice:
Come to give light
to those who are seated in the shadow of death,
  Come, O Lord, come, save your people!

O King of nations,
expectation of peoples and cornerstone of the Church:
Come to deliver
those whom you have created,
  Come, O Lord, come, save your people!

O Emmanuel,
King and hope of nations
and Savior of all people:
Come to free us, Lord, do not delay,
  Come, O Lord, come, save your people!

THOSE TRUSTING IN YOU, O LORD

Those trusting in you, O Lord,
will never be deceived.

For the husband or the wife
who awaits the return of one who has left
and will never return,
    we pray to you, Lord.
Those trusting in you, O Lord, will never be deceived.

For parents
awaiting the return of a child
who will never return,
    we pray to you, Lord.
Those trusting in you, O Lord, will never be deceived.

For those who are in prison
awaiting their return home
though they will never return,
    we pray to you, Lord.
Those trusting in you, O Lord, will never be deceived.

For those who are sick
and await the return of their health,
which will never return,
    we pray to you, Lord.
Those trusting in you, O Lord, will never be deceived.

For those who are yearning to die
yet see no end to their suffering,
    we pray to you, Lord.
Those trusting in you, O Lord, will never be deceived.

For the people of Israel
who are still awaiting the Savior
because, in Jesus, they see not his presence,
    we pray to you, Lord.
Those trusting in you, O Lord, will never be deceived.

For those who no longer are waiting for anything,
who do not even know there is a Savior to hope for,
    we pray to you, Lord.
Those trusting in you, O Lord, will never be deceived.

Psalm 25: 3,6.

Lord, God of all trust,
remember your kindness,
remember your love.

Do not deceive, Lord,
those whom life has always deceived
and whose hope is now only in you.
Keep them in the joy of your love,
O you God of all wonders,
who alone can grant our desires
beyond even hope.

HOW LONG THE WAY!

Emmanuel, come, save your people.

How long the path which leads to you!
      Lord, come to meet us,
      be our way.

How heavy the burden of our misery!
      Lord, come to meet us,
      be our rest.

How darkly hard the journey to our star!
      Lord, come to meet us,
      be our sunlight.

How lonely do we wander,
stumbling together in the darkness!
      Lord, come to meet us,
      be our brother.

How long, Lord Jesus, do we wait for your return!
Yet, since you lit hope's flame within our hearts,
come now at last to be our hope's fulfillment.
Allow us to dwell near your heart:
      there we belong
      forever and ever.

IT WILL BE DAYLIGHT SOON

The night passes on,
it will be morning soon.

The hour has come, Lord:
wake us from our sleep.

Allow us to walk with children of light
toward your coming Dawn.

THAT WE MAY BE READY

God, our Father, we pray to you:

Let your grace keep us awake
that our hearts be not dulled
    by the cares of life.

Grant us also to pray always
    that we may be standing ready
when the Son of Man comes.

LIKE DIRTY LAUNDRY

See, Lord —
our acts of goodness are before you
    like dirty laundry,
and we fall like dead leaves
    that the wind sweeps away.

But you are our Father —
how could you forget us?
Open the heavens and come down!
    Come to save us
    through your Son Jesus.

It Will Be Daylight Soon, *Romans 13:11-14,* First Sunday, A.
That We May Be Ready, *Luke 21:34-36,* First Sunday, C.
Like Dirty Laundry, *Isaiah 63:19; 64:5-7,* First Sunday, B.

STAY AWAKE AND PRAY

Lord Jesus, you tell us
to stay awake and pray
because we know
    neither the day nor the hour.

Make each day find us more ready
to welcome you into our lives,
and may the last of our days
    be the happiest,
because we will then return home
and discover the place
that you have prepared for us.

YOUR KINGDOM COME

God our Father:

Your Kingdom come
on earth as in heaven!

May the day come when the morning star
will rise in our hearts!

May the day come when we will see you face to face:
    you, our Father,
with Jesus, our Lord and our brother,
and the Spirit, which dwells in our hearts!

Stay Awake and Pray, *Matthew 24:42,* First Sunday, A.
Your Kingdom Come, *2 Peter 1:19 1 John 3:2.*

YOUR RETURN IS NEAR

"Yes, your return is near!
Oh yes, come, Lord Jesus!"

Soon I am going to see you, O my God,
and I rejoice for that day.

Not for what I am,
not for what I have,
but just because I am nothing
and my hands are empty before you.

Because I depend on you, Lord,
and I rejoice for that great feastday
when my misery will meet
your mercy.

LOVE AND TRUTH EMBRACE

In you, Lord, Jesus, tiny Babe of Bethlehem,
    love and truth now meet,
    justice and peace now embrace.
In you, Lord, truth reaches up from earth,
    and justice leans down from heaven.
        Therefore we pray:

Upon this earth, which now is yours,
may every moment of our lives unfold the mystery
    of love and truth,
    of justice and peace.

Your Return Is Near, *Revelation 22:20.*
Love and Truth Embrace, *Psalm 85:11-12,* Second Sunday, B.

THE PATH OF YOUR RETURN

Lord Jesus,
may you yourself prepare
in the wilderness of our hearts
the path of your return.

The hills of our pride —
tear them down with your humility.
The valleys of our despair —
fill them with your hope.
The winding roads of our lives —
straighten them with your truth,
and let bloom in our desert
    the daffodils of your joy.

Then will we be able to see your glory
    and adore your presence
in the face of each of our brothers and sisters.

AS THE LABORER

Lord Jesus,
you who wait at the gates,
you who are so near to us,
    we pray to you:

Lock deep in our hearts the treasure of patience
until the day of your coming, Lord.

As the laborer waits patiently
    for the precious fruit of the ground,
let us likewise wait,
    in the peace of hope,
for the time of the eternal harvest.

The Path of Your Return, *Isaiah 40:3-5,* Second Sunday, B.
As the Laborer, *James 5:7-9,* Third Sunday, A.

YOUR PEACE BEYOND ALL UNDERSTANDING

God our Father, we pray to you:
Let your peace which is far beyond all understanding
keep our hearts and our thoughts
in expectation of the return of your Son,
Jesus Christ, our Lord.

HE WHOM NO ONE CAN AWAIT

God our Father,
you are the one we cannot await,
if you yourself do not light the flame in our hearts.

You are the one we cannot desire,
if you yourself do not dwell already in our hearts.

Therefore we pray:
Each day revive in us more and more
the consciousness of our misery,
and fill us unceasingly with your mercy.

Your Peace beyond All Understanding, *Philippians 4:7,* Third Sunday, C.

BLESSINGS FOR THE ADVENT SEASON

May the God of hope fill us
with all the joy and the peace of our faith,
so that we may abound in hope
    by the power of the Holy Spirit!   —*Amen.*

May God our Father strengthen us until the last day
    so that we will be without blame
    in the Day of our Lord Jesus Christ.   —*Amen.*
He is faithful, he who calls us
to fellowship with his Son Jesus, our Lord.   —*Amen.*
To him be glory forever!   —*Amen.*

Marana tha! Come, Lord Jesus!   —*Amen.*
Your grace be with us all.   —*Amen.*

May God our Father,
who has begun an excellent work in us,
see that it is completed
when the Day of Christ Jesus comes!   —*Amen.*
To him be glory forever!   —*Amen.*

May the Lord help us to grow and abound
    in love for one another.   —*Amen.*
May he confirm our hearts in holiness without blame
    before God our Father,
at the time of his coming with all his saints!   —*Amen.*

May the God of peace himself
make us completely holy.   —*Amen.*
May he keep us blameless in spirt, soul and body,
for the coming of our Lord Jesus Christ.   —*Amen.*
Forever faithful is he who calls us — God our Father!   —*Amen.*

Expectant, let us live in joyful hope
for the revelation of the glory
of our God and Savior, Christ Jesus!   —*Amen.*
To him be glory forever!   —*Amen.*

Romans 15:13   1 Corinthians 1:8-9; 16:23-24   Philippians 1:6
1 Thessalonians 3:12-13; 5:23-24   Titus 2:12-14.

May we grow in grace and knowledge
of our Lord and Savior Jesus Christ.   —*Amen.*
To him be glory now and in eternity!   —*Amen.*

Amen! Come, Lord Jesus!   —*Amen.*
May your grace be with us all!   —*Amen.*

Each blessing concludes with the usual formula:

May almighty God bless you,
the Father, and the Son, and the Holy Spirit. Amen.

2 Peter 3:18   Revelation 22:21.

CHRISTMAS

AND

EPIPHANY

YOU WHO WISHED TO BE BORN
IN THE MIDST OF OUR SINS

Litany of the Kyrie

You are holy,
you who wished to be born in the midst of our sins
the better to pardon us,
    we beg you:
    Lord, have mercy.

You are strong,
you who wished to be born weak as a child
in order to give us strength,
    we beg you:
    Christ, have mercy.

You are immortal,
you who took on a body to die
in order to give us immortality,
    we beg you:
    Lord, have mercy.

Holy God, strong God, immortal God,
give the peace of heaven to our earth,
and open the door of your mercy
to the beggars of your love.

TODAY THE ANGELS

Glory to God on high!

Today the angels sing in the heavens —
    sing with them!
Glory to God on high!

Today the shepherds come to Bethlehem —
    come with them!
Glory to God on high!

They find Joseph and Mary and the newborn child —
    search with them!
Glory to God on high!

They marvel and give glory to God
for all that they have seen and heard —
    give glory to God!
Glory to God on high!

They proclaim the word that has been told them
concerning the Savior, Messiah, and Lord —
    proclaim Jesus with them!
Glory to God on high!

The Virgin Mary treasures all these things
and ponders them in her heart —
    pray with her!
Glory to God on high!

MAY THEY GIVE YOU GLORY FOR US, O LORD

Praise to you now and evermore!

May they give you glory for us, O Lord —
the Virgin Mary whose child you were,
and the carpenter Joseph who made you his own.
        Praise to you now and evermore!

May they give you glory for us, O Lord —
the angels who, singing, praised your birth,
and the manger wherein, as a child, you lay.
        Praise to you now and evermore!

May they give you glory for us, O Lord —
the shepherds who came to worship you,
and your mother herself, who marvelled at you.
        Praise to you now and evermore!

May they give you glory for us, O Lord —
the Bethlehem infants who died for you,
and the martyrdom of the hearts of their mothers.
        Praise to you now and evermore!

May they give you glory for us, O Lord —
the Wise Men who journeyed from far in the East,
and their brilliant star aloft in your sky.
        Praise to you now and evermore!

May they give you glory for us, O Lord —
old Simeon holding you clasped in his arms,
and Anna the prophetess,
whose age your coming did bless with joy.
        Praise to you now and evermore!

On this day [at this time] of your holy birth,
O Jesus Lord, we pray to you:
Let all our lives bring glory to you,
and because your birth was here on earth,
give us someday our own birth in heaven
        for one eternal Christmas.

O GOD, THE RULER OF AGES ETERNAL

Praise to you, O Lord!

O God, the ruler of ages eternal,
though without beginning or end,
you chose to be born an infant in time.
    Praise to you, O Lord!

O God, the invisible,
you are he whom nobody has seen or can see,
yet you assume the face of the Son of Mary.
    Praise to you, O Lord!

O God, the all-powerful,
you hold the mountains in the palm of your hand,
yet you let yourself be wrapped in swaddling clothes.
    Praise to you, O Lord!

O God, the eternal glory,
innumerable angels acclaim you endlessly,
yet you chose to be rocked to sleep
by the songs of the daughter of David.
    Praise to you, O Lord!

O God, the universal provider,
you feed every creature,
yet you chose to hunger for the milk of your Mother.
    Praise to you, O Lord!

O God, the infinite,
heaven and earth cannot contain you,
yet you rest in the arms of Mary.
    Praise to you, O Lord!

O God, the perfect joy,
you are the source of the happiness of heaven and earth,
yet you cry like a little child.
    Praise to you, O Lord!

O God, the eternal Word,
you are the light of all created intelligence,
yet you are laid in a manger
and cannot even speak.
    Praise to you, O Lord!

FOR ALL WHO GIVE YOU A FACE

Glory to God on high!

For all who give you a face,
    Lord Jesus,
by spreading your love in the world,
    we praise you.

For all who give you hands,
    Lord Jesus,
by doing their best toward their brothers and sisters,
    we praise you.

For all who give you a mouth,
    Lord Jesus,
by defending the weak and the oppressed,
    we praise you.

For all who give you eyes,
    Lord Jesus,
by seeing every bit of love
in the heart of man and woman,
    we praise you.

For all who give you a heart,
    Lord Jesus,
by preferring the poor to the rich,
the weak to the strong,
    we praise you.

For all who give to your poverty,
    Lord Jesus,
the look of hope for the Kingdom,
    we praise you.

For all who reveal you
simply by what they are,
    Lord Jesus,
because they reflect your beauty in their lives,
    we praise you.

God our Father,
you who are the God of a thousand faces,
yet whom nothing can reveal completely
except the face of the child of Bethlehem,
    we pray to you:

Continue in our lives the mystery of Christmas.
Let your Son become flesh in us
so that we may be for all our brothers and sisters
    the revelation of your love.

CHRIST SHOWN FORTH IN THE FLESH

Glory and praise to you,
Lord Jesus Christ!

Christ, shown forth in the flesh,
    Glory and praise to you!
Christ, made just in the Spirit,
    Glory and praise to you!
Christ, who was seen by the angels,   '
    Glory and praise to you,
        Lord Jesus Christ!

Christ, proclaimed among the nations,
    Glory and praise to you!
Christ, received in faith through all the world,
    Glory and praise to you!
Christ, exalted in glory,
    Glory and praise to you,
        Lord Jesus Christ!

1 Timothy 3:16.

FOR ALL THE CHILDREN OF THE WORLD

Remember us, O Lord, in your loving care.

For all the children everywhere in the world,
that they may find, like the child Jesus,
the love of a father or a mother to welcome them,
　　　let us pray.

For children who suffer from the wickedness of others,
who are hurt by their hatred or killed by their wars,
that they may find peace and joy close to God, our Father,
　　　let us pray.

For children who are born infirm,
with a deformed body or a deficient mind,
that they may find beauty of heart
close to God, the source of all splendor,
　　　let us pray.

For children who are neither wanted nor loved,
that they may know that God their Father
loves them as no one on earth can love them,
　　　let us pray.

For children who are orphans,
that they may discover in a family who adopts them
the love of their Father in heaven,
　　　let us pray.

For all children who are born of a beautiful love
and who are happy during Christmastime,
that they may learn to share their happiness,
　　　let us pray.

　　　God our Father,
source of all fatherhood in heaven and on earth,
　　　we pray to you:

Let your love watch over all the children of the world;
let it help them grow in grace and wisdom.

Keep in us, too, a childlike spirit and humility
that we may one day enter your Kingdom.

We ask this of you in the name of Jesus,
who was born for us, a little child in Bethlehem,
and who rules with you forever.

ON THIS DAY OF YOUR BIRTH

On this day [at this time] of your birth, Lord Jesus,
wonderful and adorable child,
we want to praise you and thank you.

You are the unapproachable God,
yet the shepherds meet you in the stable.
No tongue can pronounce your name,
yet Mary calls you "My little one."
You are raised above the heavens,
yet you rest in a manger.
You are the light of all lights,
yet you are born in the nighttime of humankind.

With the angels and shepherds
we surround your manger and sing:
"Glory to God in the highest,
and peace to those whom you love!"

And because you chose to make yours the sorrows
        of our humanity,
give us a share also in the riches of your divinity,
O you, the firstborn of the Virgin Mary,
        and our brother.

ONLY SON, FULL OF GRACE AND TRUTH

(Prologue of John)

Lord Jesus, only Son,
full of grace and truth,
    we pray to you:

You are the Word of your Father —
    reveal him to us!

You are the light that shines in the darkness —
    enlighten us!

You have come into the midst of your own —
    dwell among us!

You give us the power of becoming children of God —
    receive us as brothers and sisters!

You set up your tent among us —
    stay with us!

You are the Son, full of grace and truth —
    save us!

Eternal and almighty God,
King of kings and Lord of lords,
the one who alone is immortal,
the one who lives in unapproachable light,
the one whom nobody has seen or can see:

You reveal yourself today in the face
of the little child of Bethlehem.

        Thanks to you, O Lord, thanks,
        forever!

John 1:1-18   1 Timothy 5:15-16.

TODAY THE WISE MEN COME TO BETHLEHEM

Glory and praise to you,
Lord Jesus Christ!

Today the Wise Men come to Bethlehem.
    With them, Lord,
we come to render homage to you.
Glory and praise to you, Lord Jesus Christ!

Today the star leads them to the manger.
    With them, Lord,
we wish to let ourselves be led by your light.
Glory and praise to you, Lord Jesus Christ!

Today they see the little child and Mary his mother.
    With them, Lord,
we wish to discover you in the midst of our brothers and sisters.
Glory and praise to you, Lord Jesus Christ!

Today they prostrate themselves before you and adore you.
    With them, Lord,
we wish to adore your holy will for us.
Glory and praise to you, Lord Jesus Christ!

Today they offer him their gifts.
    With them, Lord,
we wish to offer you our own lives as a gift.
Glory and praise to you, Lord Jesus Christ!

On this day [at this time] of your holy birth,
O Jesus Lord, we pray to you:
Let all our lives bring glory to you.
And because your birth was here on earth,
give us someday our own birth in heaven
    for one eternal Christmas.

YOUR STAR LED THE WISE MEN

Lord Jesus,
King of kings and Lord of lords,
infant born of the Virgin Mary,
your star led the Wise Men to the manger
and they paid homage to you in your mother's arms.
    We pray to you:

For each person, light this star —
a reason for hope and for love —
a star that rises in the heavens of our hearts
and leads to you.

Together with the Wise Men,
we can then offer you as gifts
the gold of our faithfulness,
the incense of our prayer,
and the myrrh of our sacrifice.

BLESSINGS FOR CHRISTMAS AND EPIPHANY

Glory to God in the highest
and peace to those who enjoy his favor!   —*Amen.*

May you be blest, God our Father!   —*Amen.*
The mystery kept secret for endless ages
you make known today to all nations
    through your Son Jesus Christ!   —*Amen.*
Glory to you forever!   —*Amen.*

Christ, visible in the flesh,   —*Amen.*
Christ, who was seen by the angels,   —*Amen.*
Christ, proclaimed among the nations.   —*Amen.*

See how God our Father has shown his love
    in his Son Jesus Christ
for the salvation of all people!   —*Amen.*
To him be glory forever!   —*Amen.*

    In this Christmas season
see how God manifests his goodness
and his love for all people
    in his Son Jesus Christ!   —*Amen.*
He saves us not because of our merits
    but according to his mercy.   —*Amen.*
To him be glory forever!   —*Amen.*

    Blest be God, our Lord!   —*Amen.*
After having spoken in the past to our fathers
    through the prophets,
he speaks to us in our own time through his Son,
    born for us of the Virgin Mary.   —*Amen.*

Each blessing concludes with the usual formula:

    May almighty God bless you,
    the Father, and the Son, and the Holy Spirit. Amen.

Luke 2:14   Romans 16:25-26   1 Timothy 3:16   Titus 2:11; 3:4-5   Hebrews 1:1-3.

LENT

AND

PASSIONTIDE

PRAYER OF THE EXODUS

Deliver us, O Lord!

Of old, you freed your people
    from the servitude of Egypt.
Liberate us today, we beg you,
    from the slavery of sin.

Of old, you fed your people in the desert
    with the manna from heaven.
Nourish us today, we beg you,
    with the bread of eternal life.

Of old, you gave your thirsty people
    the water springing from the rock.
Quench our thirst today, we beg you,
    with the water welling up to eternal life.

Of old, you gave your people at Sinai
    the commandments of the Covenant.
Give us today, we beg you,
    your grace and your truth.

Of old, you led your people in march
    by Moses, your servant.
Lead your Church today, we beg you,
    by Jesus Christ, your Son.

Of old, you opened to your people
    a door of hope in the promised land.
Open to us today, we beg you,
    the new heavens and the new earth.

Blessed are you, God our Father,
who calls us from this land of pain
to the homeland of your joy!

As your Son Jesus Christ
passed from this world to your reign,
he loved us to the end.
Teach us to imitate this perfect love
and, by his cross and passion,
to reach the promised land of his resurrection.

John 1:17; 4:14; 6:32-33; 10:1-16; 13:1.

PENITENTIAL LITANY

Gospel of Luke

With the publican of the Gospel, let us say:
O God, be merciful to me, a sinner!

You come to look for the lost sheep;
joyfully you carry it on your shoulders —
    we beg you:
O God, be merciful to me,
    a sinner!

You go to meet the prodigal son;
you clasp him in your arms and kiss him —
    we beg you:
O God, be merciful to me,
    a sinner!

You choose as your apostle Matthew the tax-collector;
you have not come to call the righteous, but sinners —
    we beg you:
O God, be merciful to me,
    a sinner!

You enter the house of Zachaeus the tax-collector
in order to seek out and save what was lost —
    we beg you:
O God, be merciful to me,
    a sinner!

You accept the ointment of the sinful woman;
because of her tears you pardon and defend her —
    we beg you:
O God, be merciful to me,
    a sinner!

To the good thief who implores you,
you open the gate of Paradise —
    we beg you:
O God, be merciful to me,
    a sinner!

Luke 5:27-32; 7:36-50; 15; 19:1-10; 23:39-43.

THE FAST THAT I LIKE, SAYS THE LORD

Help us to fast, O Lord, by loving one another.

"The fast that I like," says the Lord,
"is the breaking of the chains of evil,
the untying of the bonds of slavery."
    Help us to fast, O Lord,
      by loving our brothers and sisters.

"It is freeing the oppressed,
and welcoming the poor into your home."
    Help us to fast, O Lord,
      by loving our brothers and sisters.

"It is clothing the person you find naked,
and not despising your neighbor."
    Help us to fast, O Lord,
      by loving our brothers and sisters.

"Then will your light shine like the dawn,
and your wound be quickly healed over."
    Help us to fast, O Lord,
      by loving our brothers and sisters.

"Then, if you cry, God will answer;
if you call, he will say: I am here."
    Help us to fast, O Lord,
      by loving our brothers and sisters.

Isaiah 58:6-10.

I HAVE SPENT MY LIFE, LORD

Lord, have mercy.

I have spent my life, Lord,
tuning up my lyre
instead of singing to you.
    I am sorry, Lord.

I have spent my life, Lord,
looking for my own path
instead of walking with you.
    I am sorry, Lord.

I have spent my life, Lord,
begging for love
instead of loving you in my brothers and sisters.
    I am sorry, Lord.

I have spent my life, Lord,
fleeing the night
instead of saying: You are my light.
    I am sorry, Lord.

I have spent my life, Lord,
seeking security
instead of placing my hand in yours.
    I am sorry, Lord.

I have spent my life, Lord,
making resolutions
and not keeping them.
    I am sorry, Lord.

Now, if it is true, Lord,
that you save us
not because of our works
but because of your great mercy,
then we are now ready
to receive your salvation.

Ephesians 2:4-10.

BY ONE MAN'S DISOBEDIENCE

It is by the disobedience of one man,
    the first Adam,
that sin entered into the world,
and, through sin, death touches all of us.

It is by the obedience of one man also,
    Christ Jesus,
that we are led to the justice
    that gives life.

We pray to you, God our Father:
Since we all bear the wound of original sin,
let us also share in the original grace
    of Jesus, your Son.

Wherever our sin is multiplied,
let the grace of your Son abound.

CONSIDER OUR WEAKNESS, LORD

Consider our weakness, Lord!

The evil that we do not want,
    we do,
and the good that we desire,
    we do not do.

Accept the offering of our goodwill.
We ask you, Lord,
    not for victory without battle,
    not for peace without war,
but simply that you do not let us fight alone
and that we may be able to love you despite our weakness.

If your mercy is our strength,
then our battle will be your victory,
    in your Son Jesus Christ.

By One Man's Disobedience, *Romans 5:12-21,* First Sunday, A.
Consider Our Weakness, Lord, *Romans 7:14-20.*

THE TEMPTATION OF JESUS

Lead us not into temptation,
but deliver us from evil!

Lord Jesus, you told us:
"Not on bread alone is man to live
but on every utterance that comes from the mouth of God."
We pray to you:
Help us during this season of Lent
to live more abundantly by your Word.
Help us also not to give into the temptation
of expecting a miracle to give us free bread
when we can earn it by our work.

Lead us not into temptation,
but deliver us from evil!

Then it was said to you:
"He will bid his angels take care of you;
with their hands they will support you
that you may never stumble on a stone."
We pray to you:
Help us never to lack confidence in your protection.
Help us also not to fall into the temptation
of asking for the miraculous help of angels
when we ourselves can move the stones from our road.

Lead us not into temptation,
but deliver us from evil!

Also you told us:
"You shall do homage to the Lord your God;
him alone shall you adore."
We pray to you:
Remove from our hearts the attraction of idols,
because you alone are our Lord and Master.
Help us also, in our adoration of you,
not to fall into the temptation
of forgetting to serve and help our brothers and sisters.

Lead us not into temptation,
but deliver us from evil!

Matthew 4:1-11, First Sunday, A.

Lord Jesus,
you have become like one of us,
you have suffered the test of temptation,
we pray to you:
Be our merciful and faithful high priest,
come to the aid of those who fall,
and deliver us from evil!

PRAYER TO THE TRANSFIGURED CHRIST

With Peter, James, and John,
lead us up on a high mountain
where we will be able to gaze upon you,
O transfigured Christ!

With Moses and Elijah, your servants,
welcome us into your glory
and speak to us about your Father.

With the apostles, as you wake us from our dreams,
allow us to raise our eyes to you
and see you alone, Jesus.

O only Son, full of grace and truth,
allow us one day to hear
the voice of your Father saying to us from heaven,
"You too are my beloved sons
whom I have given all my love."

Then our lives will be transfigured
in eternity.

The Temptation of Jesus, *Hebrews 2:17-18.*
Prayer to the Transfigured Christ, *Matthew 17:1-9 Mark 9:2-10 Luke 9:28-36,*
Second Sunday. *See also* Like Abraham, p. 146, Second Sunday, A, *and* The
Firstborn of Many, p. 132.

I WILL ANSWER HIM WHO CALLS UPON ME

To the one who loves you, Lord,
and who takes refuge under your wings,
    you promise in the psalm:

"He shall call upon me, and I will answer him;
I will be with him in distress...."

We pray to you: fulfill your promise.
Here we are in distress:
    stay by our side!
To you we cry:
    save us
through Jesus Christ, our Redeemer
    and our brother.

PRAYER FOR OUR BODIES

We pray to you, Lord, for our bodies.

    You have given them to us
to reveal ourselves to one another,
to communicate with our brothers and sisters,
to express our internal adoration of you.

Do not ever deprive us of them.
They are our earthly dwelling places:
transfigure them into eternal dwelling places
    on the day of your return.

They are our bodies of misery today:
transform them into images of your glorified body
    on the day of your resurrection.

They are disfigured by suffering and death:
dress them in the garment of your splendor
    for the feast of the new heavens
    and the new earth.

I Will Answer Him Who Calls upon Me, *Psalm 91:15,* First Sunday, C.
Prayer for Our Bodies, *2 Corinthians 5:1-4 Philippians 3:20-21,* Second
Sunday, C.

THE MAN BORN BLIND

Lord Jesus,
you opened the eyes of the man born blind,
you revealed yourself to him as Savior —
We, blindlike, extend our hands to you
    and pray:

Behold the shadows that descend on our minds:
    Enlighten us!
See how night falls in our hearts:
    Save us!

Send your Holy Spirit upon us.
May he illumine the eyes of our hearts
so that we also might recognize you
    as Savior!

May he bring the dawn of that eternal Day
when we shall see clearly
the love of your Father for each of us.

LISTEN, LORD

Listen to our prayer, Lord;
pardon our sins according to your love;
deliver us for the honor of your name.

Let the whole world know
that you are the Lord, our God,
and that we are the people who bear your name.

The Man Born Blind, *John 9 Ephesians 1:17-18 Isaiah 52:8,* Fourth Sunday, A.
See also "I Am," p. 115, Fourth Sunday, A, *and* The Seven Miracles of the Gospel
According to John, p. 90, Fourth Sunday.
Listen, Lord, *Baruch 2:14.*

YOU WHO DELIGHT IN SHOWING MERCY

Who is like you, Lord,
who always pardons sin,
who delights in showing mercy?

Once more have pity on us,
put down our faults,
throw them to the bottom of the sea!

Grant us your love and your fidelity
as you have promised to our fathers,
in the name of the love that you bear
toward your only Son, Jesus Christ,
our Savior and our brother.

FATHER OF JESUS

Father of Jesus, my brother and Savior:
    when I cry to you,
"My God, my God, why have you forsaken me?"
    do not reject me!
Recognize in my cry the voice of your Son,
and teach me to say with him,
"Father, into your hands I commend my spirit."

You Who Delight in Showing Mercy, *Micah 7:18-19.*
Father of Jesus, *Matthew 27:46 = Psalm 22:2, Luke 23:44 = Psalm 31:6.*

YOU WHO AWAIT THE RETURN OF THE SINNER

Blessed be you, O Lord, O Merciful One —
you who await the return of the sinner,
you who rejoice over finding the lost sheep,
you who embrace the son
    who returns to his home.

Bestow your mercy on all of us,
soften the hardness of our hearts,
break the pride of our impenitent spirits.

Do not close the door of your house, Lord!
Wait until the last of your children returns.
And only then begin for eternity
    the feast of your mercy!

THE TIME OF REPENTANCE

God of love,
you give your sons and daughters the fond hope
that, after sin, you leave room for repentance.

Give each of us the joy
of using this time of Lent
to return to you with all our hearts
as a child returns to his father.

You Who Await the Return of the Sinner, *Luke 15,* Fourth Sunday, C.
See also God Our Father, p. 150, Fourth Sunday, B, *and* Penitential Litany
According to Luke, p. 29, Fourth Sunday, C.
The Time of Repentance, *Wisdom 12:19.*

THE RESURRECTION OF LAZARUS

Lord Jesus,
you are the resurrection and the life.
Those who believe in you
will not die forever!
With Martha and Mary we implore you:
"Look! The one you love is ill,
he is near death!"

Lift from our hearts the sadness
that crushes them like a tombstone.
Tear from our faces the wrappings
that shroud them as garments of grief.

And when you weep at the sight of our distress
as you did at the grave of Lazarus,
we are filled with joy, Lord!
For then we know that your voice
will summon us to leave our graves
to live in the joy of your love
        forever!

OPEN OUR GRAVES

Open our graves, Lord,
remove us from the prison of death.

Place your Spirit in us
so that we may live
in a world of freedom.

The Resurrection of Lazarus, *John 11:1-45,* Fifth Sunday, A.
Open Our Graves, *Ezekiel 37:12-14,* Fifth Sunday, A.

LITANY OF THE PASSION

Have mercy, O Lord,
have mercy on us!

Lord Jesus,
in agony in the garden of Olives,
troubled by sadness and fear,
comforted by an angel:
Have mercy, O Lord, have mercy on us!

Lord Jesus,
betrayed by Judas' kiss,
abandoned by your apostles,
delivered into the hands of sinners:
Have mercy, O Lord, have mercy on us!

Lord Jesus,
accused by false witnesses,
condemned to die on the cross,
struck by servants, covered with spittle:
Have mercy, O Lord, have mercy on us!

Lord Jesus,
disowned by Peter, your apostle,
delivered to Pilate and Herod,
counted among the likes of Barabbas:
Have mercy, O Lord, have mercy on us!

Lord Jesus,
carrying your cross to Calvary,
consoled by the daughters of Jerusalem,
helped by Simon of Cyrene:
Have mercy, O Lord, have mercy on us!

Lord Jesus,
stripped of your clothes,
given vinegar to drink,
crucified with thieves:
Have mercy, O Lord, have mercy on us!

Lord Jesus,
insulted on the cross,
praying for your executioners,
pardoning the good thief:
Have mercy, O Lord, have mercy on us!

Lord Jesus,
entrusting your mother to your beloved disciple,
giving up your spirit into the hands of your Father,
dying for all of us sinners:
Have mercy, O Lord, have mercy on us!

By your sufferings, Lord,
heal the wounds in our hearts.
Let your tears be the source of joy for us,
and let your death give us life.

OUR GRIEF

Ah, Lord! Look at our grief!

Our life is like a dream
that disappears in the morning.
Our years unravel
like a garment that is wearing out.
And our thoughts are more wayward
than a ribbon of cloud
that wanders about the sky.

We humbly pray:
Give us the wisdom to number our days
not in months or years,
but simply according to how much
our love for you grows each day.

Our Grief, *Psalm 90:12* and *Psalm 102:27.*
See also Carry the Cross Each Day, p. 151.

BLESSINGS FOR THE LENTEN SEASON

May you be blessed, Lord Jesus,
who died for our sins
and rose again to give us life!   —*Amen.*
To you be glory forever!   —*Amen.*

The grace and peace of God our Father
        and the Lord Jesus Christ!   —*Amen.*
He sacrificed himself for our sins
to rescue us from this wicked world
        in accordance with the will of his Father.   —*Amen.*
To him be glory forever!   —*Amen.*

We give you thanks, our Father!
You call us to join with the saints
        and to inherit your light.   —*Amen.*
You take us out of the power of darkness
and create a place for us in the Kingdom
        of the Son of your love.   —*Amen.*
To you be glory forever!   —*Amen.*

May God grant us salvation
through our Lord Jesus Christ!   —*Amen.*
He died and arose from the dead for us,
so that, awake or asleep,
we might live together with him.   —*Amen.*

        May the God of peace,
who brought our Lord Jesus Christ back from the dead
        to become the great Shepherd of his sheep
        in the blood of a New Covenant,
help us to do his will in every kind of good deed.   —*Amen.*
May he realize in us whatever is acceptable to him
        through Jesus Christ!   —*Amen.*
To him be glory forever!   —*Amen.*

Blessed be the God and Father of our Lord Jesus Christ! —*Amen.*
In his great mercy he has given us a new birth
by raising Jesus Christ from the dead.
To him be glory forever!   —*Amen.*

Romans 4:25   Galatians 1:3-5   Colossians 1:12-13
1 Thessalonians 5:9-10   Hebrews 13:20-21   1 Peter 1:3.

May grace and peace be given us by Jesus Christ!
He is the faithful witness,
the firstborn from the dead,
the ruler of the kings of the earth.   *—Amen.*
He loves us and has washed away our sins with his blood.
He has made us a kingdom of priests
    for his God and Father.   *—Amen.*
To him be glory and power forever!   *—Amen.*

Each blessing concludes with the usual formula:

    May almighty God bless you,
    the Father, and the Son, and the Holy Spirit. Amen.

Revelation 1:5-7.

THE PASCHAL CYCLE

PROCLAIMING YOUR RESURRECTION

Jesus Christ, risen Lord,
have mercy on us!

Help us, O risen Lord,
    to proclaim your resurrection,
by bringing good news to the poor
and healing the hearts that are broken.

Help us, O risen Lord,
    to proclaim your resurrection,
by feeding those who are hungry
and clothing those who are naked.

Help us, O risen Lord,
    to proclaim your resurrection,
by releasing the captives of injustice
and all those who are imprisoned by their sins.

Help us, O risen Lord,
    to proclaim your resurrection,
by welcoming the strangers
and visiting those in loneliness.

Help us, O risen Lord,
    to proclaim your resurrection,
by bringing your peace to those who are in trouble
and your joy to those who are in sorrow.

God our Father,
who raised your Son from the dead,
help us to understand, we beg you,
that we conquer our own death
and rise with Jesus today
when we live in love.

We ask you this grace through Jesus Christ,
    who died for our sins
    and rose for our life.

Isaiah 61:1-2   Matthew 25:31-40   Romans 4:25.

WE REMEMBER YOU, O RISEN LORD

Alleluia, Alleluia, Alleluia!

We remember you, O risen Lord,
firstborn of the dead.
Your resurrection destroys the power of death
and changes tears of agony into cries of joy.
        Blessed are you!

We remember you, O risen Lord,
new springtime in our life.
Your resurrection covers the fields with flowers
and brings the new creation into our hearts.
        Blessed are you!

We remember you, O risen Lord,
new Exodus from the land of sin.
Your resurrection gives us the signal
for a new departure in a life of grace.
        Blessed are you!

We remember you, O risen Lord,
new Moses on the mountain.
Your resurrection opens the gates
of the new heavens and the new earth.
        Blessed are you!

We remember you, O risen Lord,
Prophet of the messianic time.
Your resurrection initiates the law
of the new love with a renewed heart.
        Blessed are you!

We remember you, O risen Lord,
New Covenant at the feast of the cross.
Your resurrection dresses the table
for the bread of heaven and the cup of salvation.
        Blessed are you!

Luke 1:78   1 Corinthians 5:7   2 Timothy 1:10   Revelation 1:5; 21:1-5.

BY YOUR RESURRECTION

Alleluia, Alleluia, Alleluia!

By your resurrection, O Lord,
you become the firstborn of the dead.
Help us live the newness of your life.

By your resurrection
you seal the New Covenant.
Place in our hearts your own Spirit.

By your resurrection
you killed hate among people.
Help us live the new law of your love.

By your resurrection
you clothed yourself with immortality.
Help us put on the New Man
created in justice and holiness of truth.

By your resurrection
you sit at the right hand of your Father.
Help us discover in the earthly realities
the path to your heavenly Kingdom.

By your resurrection
you restore the universe.
Rebuild also your Church in your joy,
because the life of your risen people
is the witness of your resurrection.

Philippians 2:16   Ephesians 4:24   Colossians 3:1-2
Hebrews 8:7-13   Revelation 21:5.

THIS IS THE DAY YOU HAVE MADE FOR US

This is the day you have made for us,
> risen Lord,
a day of happiness and joy!

We pray to you, Lord:
Make each day that you give us
the most beautiful day of our lives,
because it is the day you have chosen
for us to encounter you,
> O risen Christ!

YOUR RESURRECTION IS THE HOPE OF OUR OWN

May you be blessed, Lord Jesus,
because your resurrection is the hope of our own,
and the glory that will clothe us on the last day
is a reflection of that which clothed you
> on Easter morning.

We pray to you:
Let all our lives express this hope
by their constant renewal through the joy of your love
> and the service of our brothers and sisters.

TO TESTIFY TO YOUR RESURRECTION

May you be blessed, Lord Jesus,
you who call us to testify to your resurrection
> unto the ends of the earth!
> But come to our aid,
so that our testimony may be worthy of you.

You wish us to proclaim that you are living,
though we ourselves fear death.

This Is the Day You Have Made for Us, *Psalm 118.*
Your Resurrection Is the Hope of Our Own, *Colossians 3:1-4.*

You wish us to announce your light,
though we grope in the darkness.

You command us to speak with authority,
though we stutter in ignorance before your mystery.

You wish us to affirm your free gift of mercy for all people,
though we have to beg for it, first of all, for ourselves.

You wish to make us God's assistants,
though we carry the weight of our own fatigue.

Can anything make so many contradictions work together
        except your love alone?
A love that calls us in spite of our faults,
that gives us confidence in spite of our unfaithfulness!

To you be glory, O wonderful Christ,
with the Father and the Holy Spirit,
        forever!

YOU RAISE US UP WITH CHRIST

May you be blessed, Lord, God our Father!

When we are dead because of our sins,
you give us new life with Christ;
with him you raise us up,
with him you make us reign in heaven.

We pray to you: help us to live from now on
no longer as strangers to the Kingdom,
but as people familiar with the house of God.

Let all our resurrected life announce
the love that you offer all people
and the joy with which you brighten all lives,
through your Son Jesus Christ,
who is our life and our resurrection
        forever.

Ephesians 2:5-6, 19.

MY LORD AND MY GOD!

Lord Jesus,
you appeared to your apostles after the resurrection
and filled their hearts with joy when you said to them,
    "Peace be with you!"

Come also into the midst of this community.
Bring it the peace of your presence,
and may your joy overflow our hearts
    like the springtime sun.
Then with your apostle Thomas we will greet you
    with a joyful shout:
    "My Lord and my God!"

VICTORY OVER THE WORLD

Lord Jesus, your apostle tells us:
"This is the victory over the world —
    our faith!"

    We pray to you:
Increase our faith
so that we might, first of all, triumph
    over our own unbelief.

Grant that our victory over the world
will be to serve those who do not believe.
Make our victory so beautifully humble
that they will wish to join us.
Let them also come to triumph over themselves
by becoming children of God
    through faith.

My Lord and My God! *John 20:19-20.*
Victory over the World, *1 John 5:1-6.*

UNITED HEART AND SOUL

Lord Jesus, your resurrection has brought together
the multitude of believers into a single community.
     We pray:

May your Church of today, like that of old,
          have but one heart,
          but one soul.

In the unity of its faith in you
and its love for its brothers and sisters,
may it bear witness to your resurrection
with the power of the Holy Spirit.

STAY WITH US, LORD

Walk with us, Lord,
along the road of resurrection!

Explain for us, so slow to believe,
the things that Scripture says of you.

Break the bread of the Eucharist with us
whenever we share our lives
          with our brothers and sisters.

     Stay with us
each time night approaches
and the daylight fades in our hearts!

United Heart and Soul, *Acts 4:32-35.*
Stay with Us, Lord, *Luke 24:13-15.*

IN EACH PAGE OF SCRIPTURE

Lord Jesus,
open our spirits to the understanding of the Scriptures
as you opened those of your apostles.
Explain to us what concerns you
in the Law of Moses, in the prophets and the psalms.

Then in each page of Scripture
we will be able to see your face,
      O risen Lord!

PUT HATRED TO DEATH

By your death, Lord Jesus, put hatred to death,
and by your resurrection, bring love back to life.

Reconcile all people with the Father;
bring together all nations
into a New Man;
destroy the barriers
that sin erects between people.

Proclaim peace to those who are far away,
and to those who are near.

Open the way of the Spirit to your Father,
you who are our life and our resurrection
      for all eternity.

In Each Page of Scripture, *Luke 24:44-45,* Third Sunday, B.
Put Hatred to Death, *Ephesians 2:14-18.*

THE GOOD SHEPHERD

Gather together your sheep, Lord,
in all the places where they have been scattered
during the mist and darkness.

Lead them to good pasturage;
let them rest in good grazing ground.

Those who are lost — search out;
those who have strayed — bring back.

Those who are wounded — bind their wounds;
those who are sick — cure.

Those bearing young — watch over them;
all of your sheep — keep them safe in your flock.

　　Lord Jesus,
because you are our good shepherd,
help us all to be the sheep of your flock.

Gather all people into the fold of your love
so that there may be but one flock
　　and one shepherd.

SUCH A SHEPHERD

Ever a shepherd who feeds his flock,
who carries the sheep in his arms,
who cradles them on his breast,
who leads the mother ewes to their rest —
such a shepherd are you for each of us, Lord.
　　May you be blest
　　forever and ever!

The Good Shepherd, *Ezekiel 34:11-16 Isaiah 40:10 John 10.*
Such a Shepherd, *Isaiah 40:10. See also* "I Am," p. 115.

WE SHALL COME TO HIM

Lord Jesus, you said:
"If anyone loves me,
he will keep my Word,
and my Father will love him;
and we shall come to him
and make our home with him."
    We pray:

Look at our misery.
We have not been faithful to the Word,
yet we dare to ask you:
    Do not abandon us,
but come make your home with us
        not because of our merits
but simply because you are merciful.

GREATER THAN OUR HEARTS

    Lord Jesus,
sometimes our hearts reproach us.
But you are greater than our hearts!

Your pardon is greater than our weakness;
your joy lessens our anguish,
and your strength overcomes our distress.

Keep us in the assurance of your love
and our hearts will remain at peace.

We Shall Come to Him, *John 14:23-24,* Fifth Sunday, A.
Greater than Our Hearts, *1 John 3:19-20,* Fifth Sunday, B.
See also "I Am Going to Prepare a Place for You," p. 150, *and* Source of All
Joy, p. 134.

THE HOPE THAT IS IN US

God our Father, you wish us
always to be ready to answer
anyone who asks the reason
for the hope that is in us.

    We pray to you:
Place in us your Holy Spirit,
the Spirit of truth and love.

Help us to bear witness to your truth
    with the purest charity,
so that our truth may always be charitable,
full of respect for those who do not believe.

Help us also to bear witness to your love
    with a shining truth,
so that our love may always be true,
full of patience for those who do not love you.

Then we will be witnesses of your Son Jesus,
in whom love and truth dwell together.

A NEW LIFE

By your death, Lord Jesus,
make the old man die in us,
and by your resurrection,
clothe us again with the New Man,
created for holiness and truth.

Help us to abandon forever
    the oldness of sin,
so that, from now on, we will have a new life
    in the joy of your resurrection.

The Hope That Is in Us, *1 Peter 3:15-18,* Sixth Sunday, A.
A New Life, *Ephesians 4:24.*

THE ASCENSION

Jesus Christ,
Lord glorified on high,
look with love upon your brothers and sisters on earth.

Your ascension is the hope
of our future glory,
and your presence near your Father
announces our own entrance into the eternal dwelling.

We pray to you:
Let the desire for heavenly realities
not make us neglect our work on earth.

Let our hope for the future
inspire in us a respect for the present moment.

Let your ascension into heaven move us
to make your glory dwell on earth.

Thus we will be witnesses to your presence
among our brothers and sisters
until the end of time.

Acts 1:8   Ephesians 2:6.

NEAR HIM IN YOUR KINGDOM

God our Father,
you who have raised your Son Jesus Christ
    from among the dead,
    we pray to you:

Raise us with him;
place us near him in your Kingdom.

Allow us to carry in our bodies
the suffering and death of Jesus
so that the life itself of Jesus
may always be seen in our mortal flesh.

And when our earthly dwelling is destroyed,
give us the everlasting home
that was not built by human hands
but that your love has built for us
    in heaven.

We ask this of you through your Son Jesus Christ,
him who is our life and our resurrection,
in the love of the Holy Spirit,
    forever.

WE PASS FROM DEATH TO LIFE

We know that we pass
    from death to life
when we love our brothers and sisters.

Grant us, then, Lord Jesus,
    from this very moment
to rise from the dead with you
    by loving our brothers and sisters
    as you love us.

Near Him in Your Kingdom, *2 Corinthians 4:10-14; 5:1 John 11:25.*
We Pass from Death to Life, *1 John 3:14.*

BLESSINGS FOR THE EASTER SEASON

May you be blessed, Lord Jesus,
who died for our sins
and rose again for our life!   —*Amen.*
To you be glory forever!   —*Amen.*

Let us give thanks to God, who gives us victory
through our Lord Jesus Christ!   —*Amen.*

Blessed be God our Father,
who raised his Son Jesus Christ to life!   —*Amen.*
He will raise us one day with him
and will place us together by his side!   —*Amen.*

May God grant us salvation
through our Lord Jesus Christ!   —*Amen.*
He died and arose from the dead for us
so that, awake or asleep,
we might live together with him.   —*Amen.*
To him be glory forever!   —*Amen.*

Jesus Christ: the same,
yesterday, today, and forever.   —*Amen.*
To him be glory and honor
forever and ever.   —*Amen.*

May the God of peace
who brought our Lord Jesus Christ back from the dead
to become the great Shepherd of the sheep
in the blood of a New Covenant,
help us to do his will in every kind of work.   —*Amen.*
May he realize in us everything that is pleasing to him,
through Jesus Christ!   —*Amen.*
To him be glory forever!   —*Amen.*

Blessed be the God and Father of our Lord Jesus Christ! —*Amen.*
In his great mercy, he has given us a new birth
by raising Jesus Christ from the dead.   —*Amen.*

Romans 4:25 1 Corinthians 15:57 2 Corinthians 4:14
1 Thessalonians 5:9-10 Hebrews 13:8, 20-21 1 Peter 1:3.

May grace and peace be given us by Jesus Christ!   *—Amen.*
He is the faithful witness,
the firstborn from the dead,
the ruler of the kings of the earth.   *—Amen.*
He loves us and redeems us from our sins by his blood.
He makes us a kingdom of priests
      for his God and Father.   *—Amen.*
To him be glory and power forever!   *—Amen.*

Each blessing concludes with the usual formula:

May almighty God bless you,
the Father, and the Son, and the Holy Spirit. Amen.

Revelation 1:5-7.

PENTECOST

AND

THE CHURCH

POUR OUT YOUR SPIRIT, LORD

Pour out your Spirit, Lord, on all humankind,
as you did on the first Pentecost!

Pour out your Spirit on our sons and our daughters,
on the young and the old,
on the slaves and the servants,
on the men and the women!

May all of us become a prophetic people,
the people of Jesus!

Joel 3:1-2   Acts 2:17-18.

THE HOLY SPIRIT AND PENTECOST

The following liturgical prayers ask for the grace of the Holy Spirit.

The first recalls certain traditional elements that concern the theology of the gifts of the Holy Spirit and that are found in Isaiah 11:2 and in Galatians 5:22-23.

The second has, as its source, the texts of Scripture which manifest the presence of the Spirit in the life of Jesus.

The third uses the scriptural texts that reflect the presence of the Spirit in the ancient community as recorded in the Acts of the Apostles.

The fourth prayer, the longest of all, recalls the texts that refer to the action of the Holy Spirit according to other scriptural sources, most particularly the Epistles of St. Paul.

It is evident, however, that one must choose from among the many suggested intentions of these prayers, and that those chosen should be adapted not only to the quality of the celebrating assembly but also to the rite of the celebration. Therefore, in an ordinary celebration, it would be better to engage the attention of the assembly by moderation than by excess. Thus three or four well-chosen intentions quietly and fervently presented would serve as a greater aid to prayer than would eight or ten made with haste or thoughtlessness.

In regard to the President's Oration that concludes these prayers, it is better that it be addressed to the Father. It is the Father, in effect, who, through the Son, gives us the Holy Spirit, and it is the Spirit of Jesus Christ who leads us to the Father, the first source of all holiness, of all love, and of all joy.

For these four prayers the following responses are suggested: *Come to us, Holy Spirit! — Come to us, Spirit of Holiness! — Come to us, Spirit of the Lord!*

THE SPIRIT TOO HELPS US IN OUR WEAKNESS,
FOR WE DO NOT KNOW HOW TO PRAY AS WE OUGHT:
BUT THE SPIRIT HIMSELF MAKES INTERCESSION FOR US
WITH GROANINGS THAT CANNOT BE EXPRESSED
IN SPEECH.

Romans 8:26.

THE GIFTS OF THE SPIRIT

Let us pray to the Lord Jesus
that he place in us
the gifts of his Spirit
and the power of his love.
> *Come to us, Spirit of the Lord!*

Spirit of wisdom,
Spirit of understanding,
Spirit of adoration,
> Come to us, Spirit of the Lord!

Spirit of strength,
Spirit of knowledge,
Spirit of joy,
> Come to us, Spirit of the Lord!

Spirit of love,
Spirit of peace,
Spirit of jubilation,
> Come to us, Spirit of the Lord!

Spirit of willing service,
Spirit of goodness,
Spirit of gentleness,
> Come to us, Spirit of the Lord!

God our Father,
source of all love and joy,
you who never measure the grace of your Spirit
but offer it to every person
with the royal generosity of divine giving,
> we pray to you:

In giving us the Spirit of your Son,
pour into our hearts the fullness of love,
so that we are able to love you alone
yet preserve all our tenderness for people also,
> in this unique love,
> through Christ our Lord.
> Amen.

Isaiah 11:2   Galatians 5:22-23   John 3:34   Romans 5:5.

THE SPIRIT IN THE LIFE OF JESUS

Holy Spirit,
who came upon the Virgin Mary
so that she became the Mother of Jesus,   *Lk 1:34*
    we pray to you:
Open our hearts to your word,
help us to receive Jesus, the Word of God.

Holy Spirit,
who came upon Zechariah, Elizabeth, and Simeon,   *Lk 1:41, 67*
and helped them recognize the Messiah,   *Lk 2:26*
    we pray to you:
Enlighten the eyes of our hearts
so that we may know how to recognize Jesus, the Lord.

Holy Spirit,   *Mt 3:16*
who came upon Christ Jesus   *Mk 1:10*
when he was baptized in the waters of the Jordan,   *Lk 3:22*
    we pray to you:
Baptize us in the fire of your love
so that the Father may say to each of us: *Mt 3:17*
"You are my beloved Son.   *Lk 3:22*
On you my favor rests."

Holy Spirit,   *Mt 4:1*
who led Christ Jesus   *Mk 1:12*
out into the desert of temptation,   *Lk 4:1*
    we pray to you:
Give us the strength
to conquer in ourselves the power of evil.

Holy Spirit,
who sent Christ Jesus   *Mt 12:18-21*
to carry the Good News to the poor,   *Lk 4:18-19*
    we pray to you:
Help us to continue your work
by serving the poor, our brothers and sisters.

Holy Spirit,
who filled Christ Jesus with joy   *Lk 10:21*
and opened his mouth to praise the Father,   *Mt 11:27*
    we pray to you:
Teach us to say to him,
"Yes, Father, your gracious will be done!"

Holy Spirit,
you who speak through the mouth of despised disciples,
    we pray to you: *Mt 10:20*
Place in us your words of wisdom;   *Lk 13:11*
help us to conquer evil by good.   *Rom 12:21*

Holy Spirit,
in whom Jesus, the perfect oblation,
is offered to the love of his Father,   *Heb 9:14*
    we pray to you:
Make of us an eternal offering
in praise of your glory.   *Eph 1:14*

THE SPIRIT IN THE ACTS OF THE APOSTLES

    Let us call upon the Spirit of Jesus:
    Today, as in the time of the apostles,
    may he assist his Church
    for the glory of God the Father.

Spirit of Jesus,
poured out in flames of fire upon your disciples   *Acts 2:1-11*
on the day of Pentecost,   *(4:31)*
    we pray to you:
Set afire the hearts of your faithful
so that they will announce in all the languages of the world
the wonders of the salvation of God.

Holy Spirit,
who helped Peter before the Sanhedrin   *Acts 4:8*
when he gave testimony to Christ Jesus,
    we pray to you:
Help us to announce with confidence   *Acts 5:32*
the Good News of Jesus Christ.

Holy Spirit,
who filled Stephen the martyr with your wisdom,
who opened the heavens before him   *Acts 6:10*
and showed him Jesus
standing at the right hand of his Father,   *Acts 7:55*
    we pray to you:
Enlighten the eyes of our hearts
so that in the difficulties
and the persecutions of this world
we may know how to recognize the presence of the Lord.

Holy Spirit,
who led the deacon Philip on the road from Gaza
to the meeting with the eunuch of the queen of Ethiopia
and had him announce the Good News of Jesus,
  we pray to you: *Acts 8:26-40*
Lead your missionaries
toward all those who are seeking the truth.

Holy Spirit,
who built up the infant churches   *Acts 9:31*
and filled them with your consolation,
  we pray to you:
Make the Kingdom of God on earth
grow by your joy and your peace.

Holy Spirit,
who called Paul and Barnabas
to their mission among the pagans   *Acts 13:4*
and filled them with the joy
of announcing the Good News,   *Acts 13:52*
  we pray to you:
Today again bring to life some fervent witnesses for Christ.

Holy Spirit,
who helped the apostles at the council of Jerusalem
and inspired their decisions,   *Acts 15:28*
  we pray to you:
Enlighten those in authority
that their ministry
will be of service to their brothers and sisters. *Acts 20:28*

Holy Spirit,
you who pointed out the way for your disciples
to announce the Gospel,   *Acts 16:6-8*
  we pray to you:
As in the time of the apostles,
guide today's messengers of the Good News.

COME TO US, SPIRIT OF HOLINESS

The Spirit in the Epistles

Let us humbly call upon the Holy Spirit
so that our life in Christ Jesus
may glorify God our Father.

Spirit of Jesus,
you pour the love of God into our hearts;   *Rom 5:5*
    we pray to you:
Enflame all our lives
with the fire of your love.

Spirit of Jesus,
you help us to serve God our Father
in the new life of the Spirit
and not in the oldness of the letter;   *Rom 7:6*
    we pray to you:
When we read the Word of God,
lift the veil from our hearts   *2 Cor 3:14*
so that we will discover there the face of Jesus Christ.

Holy Spirit,
your law gives us life in Christ Jesus;   *Rom 8:3*
    we pray to you:
Free us from the law of sin and death.

Holy Spirit,
you raised Christ Jesus from the dead;   *Rom 8:11*
    we pray to you:
Stamp upon us the seal of eternal life.

Holy Spirit,
you banish fear from our hearts;
you bear witness in us that we are children of God;
    we pray to you:
Remove from our hearts the spirit of slaves;
place in us the spirit of adopted children   *Rom 8:15-17*
to make us cry out, "Abba, Father!"   *Gal 4:4*

Holy Spirit,
you come to the aid of our weakness
because we do not know how to pray as we should;   *Rom 8:26-27*
    we beg you:
Intercede for us,
and place in our hearts and on our lips
a prayer pleasing to the Father.

Spirit of Jesus,
you who are our life, *Gal 5:25*
    we pray to you:
Help us to act as children of God
who follow Christ Jesus,
the firstborn of many brothers and sisters. *Rom 8:29*

Spirit of Jesus,
you sanctified the pagans,
making them a pleasing offering to the Father;
    we pray to you:
Make us apostles of your Gospel,
ministers of Jesus Christ to the nations. *Rom 15:16*

Holy Spirit,
you know the infinite depths of God; *1 Cor 2:10-12*
    we pray to you:
Reveal to us the mystery of the Father
and the love that surpasses all knowledge. *Eph 3:19*

Spirit of Jesus,
you make us holy temples
to the glory of the Father;
    we pray to you:
Help us to glorify God in our bodies. *1 Cor 6:19-20*

Holy Spirit,
by your grace we can say:
"Jesus is Lord!" *1 Cor 12:3*
Help us to live in holiness
and thus to proclaim the kingdom of Christ Jesus.

Holy Spirit,
you distribute your gifts
for the common good of the whole Church; *1 Cor 12:4-11*
    we pray to you:
Let the variety of gifts and of ministries
strengthen the unity of the whole body
that everyone may be loved in the Church
for the special work he accomplishes.

Holy Spirit,
in you we have been baptized
to form only one Body; *1 Cor 12:13*
    we pray to you:

Gather together all Christians
in the unity of your Church.

Holy Spirit,
pledge of our inheritance,   *2 Cor 1:22; 5:5*
you set your seal on our hearts;   *Eph 1:14*
    we pray to you:
Against the day of our redemption   *Eph 4:30*
seal us with the sign of Christ.

Spirit of Jesus,
wherever you reign,   *2 Cor 3:17*
there freedom triumphs;
    we pray to you:
Lead us to the complete truth,   *Jn 16:13*
so that your truth will make us free.   *Jn 8:32*

Holy Spirit,
you unite the Church in the bond of peace;   *Eph 4:3*
    we pray to you:
End all divisions in the Body of Christ,
gather us together in your love.

Spirit of God, Spirit of glory,
you come to rest on those who are insulted   *1 Pt 4:14*
for the name of Christ Jesus;
    we pray to you:
Fill with your strength and your peace
those who suffer persecution for the Kingdom.

Spirit of truth,   *Jn 14:17*
whom the Father sends in the name of the Son,
    we pray to you:
Recall to our memories the words of Jesus
and keep them in our hearts.   *Jn 14:26*

SANCTIFY YOUR GREAT NAME

Come to us, Spirit of the Lord!

Sanctify your great name
that our life has profaned.
Come to us, Spirit of the Lord!

Show your holiness
so that the world will recognize you as God.
Come to us, Spirit of the Lord!

Gather together your children
whom sin has scattered.
Come to us, Spirit of the Lord!

Pour clean water on us;
cleanse us of all our idols.
Come to us, Spirit of the Lord!

Remove our hearts of stone;
give us new hearts.
Come to us, Spirit of the Lord!

Pour your Spirit into us
so that we will walk according to your will.
Come to us, Spirit of the Lord!

You are our God, Lord:
Make us be your people!
Come to us, Spirit of the Lord!

Ezekiel 36:23-27.

YOUR SPIRIT, LORD, IS TRUTH

Come to us, Spirit of the Lord!

Your Spirit, Lord, is truth:
May it make us free.
Come to us, Spirit of the Lord!

Your Spirit, Lord, is fire:
May it enkindle us with love.
Come to us, Spirit of the Lord!

Your Spirit, Lord, is gentleness:
May it bring us peace.
Come to us, Spirit of the Lord!

Your Spirit, Lord, renews the face of the earth:
May it renew the depths of our hearts.
Come to us, Spirit of the Lord!

Your Spirit, Lord, is prayer:
May it open our hearts to give praise.
Come to us, Spirit of the Lord!

Your Spirit, Lord, fills the whole universe:
May it live among us forever.
Come to us, Spirit of the Lord!

Your Spirit, Lord, is life:
May it raise us up on the last day.
Come to us, Spirit of the Lord!

FOR THE CHURCH OF YOUR SON JESUS

God our Father, we pray to you
for the Church of your Son Jesus.

Let her be resplendent
with the beauty of Jesus;
let her avoid painting herself
with the vain beauty of the world.

Let her not be disfigured
by the wrinkles of old age;
let her represent for all people
the hope of the future.

Let her face be purified
from every stain of pride;
let her show preference
for the poor and the humble.

Let her be holy and spotless;
let her not be maimed by error.

Let her be beautiful as one betrothed,
all dressed up for her spouse;
let her shun the unseemly "adornments"
of money and power.

Lord Jesus,
you have loved your Church,
and you have given yourself up for her;
　　we pray to you:
Guide this Church that she, in turn,
will love all people
and put herself at their service.

Ephesians 5:25-27.

LET HER REMOVE HER DRESS OF SORROW

We pray to you, God our Father,
for the Church of your Son Jesus.

May she remove her dress of sorrow;
may she put on the mantle of your justice;
may the crown of your glory sparkle on her head!

May her face shine
with the very splendor of the beauty of your Son!

In her journey toward you,
give her as escort, Lord,
your mercy and your justice.

THE TOTTERING HUT OF DAVID

Lord, God of our fathers,
you who have promised by the mouth of your prophet Amos:
"I will raise up the fallen hut of David,
wall up its breaches,
raise up its ruins,
and rebuild it as in the days of old,"
     we beg you:

See our Church that ruin threatens.
Wall up the breaches of its faults;
raise up the ruins of its love;
rebuild its faith on the rock of your Word.

Make it resplendent with the very beauty of Jesus
so that all people, tempted by its splendor,
will seek again and find in it the salvation and the joy
     of your Son Jesus Christ.

Let Her Remove Her Dress of Sorrow, *Baruch 5:1-9.*
The Tottering Hut of David, *Amos 9:11.*

GOD THE FATHER, SON, AND HOLY SPIRIT

Blest are you, O Lord,
through eternity!

God the Father,
we praise you and we bless you
because you are the Father of Jesus,
and because you wish to be our Father also
according to your love and mercy.
Blest are you, O Lord, through eternity!

God the Son,
we praise you and we bless you
because you are the Son of the Father's love,
and because you wish to be the eldest brother also
of all the children of God.
Blest are you, O Lord, through eternity!

God the Holy Spirit,
we praise you and we bless you
because you are the love of the Father and the Son,
springing up like a fire out of their affection,
and because you wish to dwell in our hearts also
like a furnace of love.
Blest are you, O Lord, through eternity!

God the Father, Son, and Holy Spirit,
we praise you and we bless you
because you are God surpassing all praise,
yet you accept the stammering
    of our adoration.
To you we direct our love forever and ever.
Blest are you, O Lord, through eternity!

BLESSED AMONG WOMEN BE THE VIRGIN MARY!
BLESSED IS JESUS, THE FRUIT OF HER LOVE!

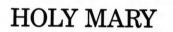

HOLY MARY

WITH THE VIRGIN MARY

With the Virgin Mary,
our souls proclaim the greatness of the Lord
and our spirits exult with joy
in Jesus our Savior.
Blest are you, O Lord,
through eternity!

Because you have looked with favor
upon your lowly handmaid,
blest are you, O Lord,
through eternity!

Because the power of your love
has done great things for her,
blest are you, O Lord,
through eternity!

Because your mercy reaches from age to age
to all who worship you,
blest are you, O Lord,
through eternity!

Because you show the power of your arm
and scatter the proud of heart,
blest are you, O Lord,
through eternity!

Because you cast down princes from their thrones
and exalt the lowly,
blest are you, O Lord,
through eternity!

Because you fill the hungry with good things
and send the rich away empty,
blest are you, O Lord,
through eternity!

Because you are mindful of the mercy
promised to our fathers,
to Abraham and to his descendants forever,
blest are you, O Lord,
through eternity!

Luke 1:46-55.

We pray to you, God our Father:
Give us souls of praise
like that of the Virgin Mary,
souls that know how to marvel at your love
and find joy in telling you, "Thanks!"

JOY TO YOU, O VIRGIN MARY

Joy to you, O Virgin Mary,
Mother of the Lord!

Humble maiden of Nazareth,
betrothed to the carpenter Joseph,
greeted by the angel Gabriel!

Lowly handmaid of the Lord,
you on whom his favor rested,
to whom, all full of grace, the Lord was present!

Lovely Mother of Abraham's Son,
exalted Mother of David's Son,
Holy Mother of Jesus the Lord!

You most blessed among all women,
of whose own womb the fruit was blessed,
you most praised by all generations!

You to whom God's Holy Spirit came,
in whom the Word became our flesh,
through whose grace he dwells among us!

You who bore your Son, laid in a manger,
while angels sang "To God on high be glory,
and peace on earth to people of goodwill!"

You whose Child was sung to by the angels,
and acclaimed in joy by the shepherds,
as you marvelled at his wondrous birth!

You who showed him to the Wise Men,
you who brought him to the temple,
you who gave joy to aged Simeon!

Chosen Mother of the Messiah,
virgin and daughter of Sion,
glory and honor of God's holy people!

Suffering Mother under the cross,
glorious Mother of the apostles,
Queen and joy of all generations!

Glorious woman clothed with the sun,
with the moon under your feet,
on your head a crown of twelve stars!

WE GREET YOU, VIRGIN MARY

We greet you, Virgin Mary,
and we bless Jesus your Child.
To him be honor and praise
    Eternally!

Holy Mary,
Holy Mother of God,
Virgin full of grace,
Pray to the Lord for us.

Mother of Christ,
Mother of divine grace,
Mother most pure,
Pray to the Lord for us.

Mother ever Virgin,
Mother worthy of love,
Admirable Mother,
Pray to the Lord for us.

Mother of good counsel,
Mother of the Creator,
Mother of our Savior,
Pray to the Lord for us.

Faithful Virgin,
Mirror of holiness,
Throne of wisdom,
Pray to the Lord for us.

Source of our joy,
Abode of the Holy Spirit,
Mystical rose,
Pray to the Lord for us.

Ark of the Covenant,
Gate of Heaven,
Morning Star,
Pray to the Lord for us.

Consolation of the afflicted,
Refuge of sinners,
Strength of Christians,
Pray to the Lord for us.

Queen of angels,
Queen of patriarchs and prophets,
Queen of apostles,
Pray to the Lord for us.

Queen of martyrs,
Queen of virgins,
Queen of all saints,
Pray to the Lord for us.

Queen conceived without sin,
Queen raised up to heaven,
Queen of peace,
Pray to the Lord for us.

Lord Jesus, Son of the Virgin Mary,
you wished that all ages
proclaim your blessed Mother.

We also wish to fulfill the prophecy
and sing the glories of your Mother.

As praise, accept our lives,
offered in the service of our brothers and sisters,
       through love for you,
Jesus, Son of Mary and our brother.

ANNUNCIATION

We bless you, God our Father,
for having loved the Virgin Mary so much.

Through her we too find favor with you
    in her Son Jesus,
who today becomes our brother.

Send down upon us your Holy Spirit
so that we too might become the temple of your glory
and that Jesus might be born in our hearts
    through faith.

For nothing is impossible for your love.

VISITATION

Blest be the Virgin Mary among women!
Blest be Jesus, her Child!
Supremely blest is God our Father,
source of all grace and all blessing!

When Mary visited her cousin Elizabeth,
she brought her the presence of Jesus,
and was for her the source of joy.

Each time that we meet our brothers and sisters,
we can likewise bring them
    the presence of Jesus Christ
and enlighten them by the radiance of his joy.

God our Father, give us the same grace
that you bestowed through the Virgin Mary
on the day of the Visitation.
We ask this of you in the name of the love
that you have for your only Son, Jesus Christ,
and in memory of his beloved Mother.

Luke 1:26-38, 39-56.

PRESENTATION OF JESUS IN THE TEMPLE

Eternal God, born a tiny child,
you were presented in the temple in the arms of Mary,
and the aged Simeon proclaimed you
light of the nations and glory of your people Israel.

Through the hands of Mary, our sister,
we present you once again, today, to your Father.

Make your light rise
like a joyous dawn upon all those
    who do not know your name.
Be the glory of Israel, your people according to the flesh,
    who still have not recognized you.

And when the evening of our life arrives,
give us a share in Simeon's joy
at being able to see you in the peace of eternity.

ASSUMPTION

Lord Jesus, Son of the Virgin Mary,
we praise you and bless you
for having so glorified your Mother
in her soul and body.

If the day of death
is the day of birth into heaven,
your Mother was never so young
as on the morning of her Assumption.

Help us to grow old as she did
while continually becoming younger,
until the day when we will be children enough
to enter the Kingdom.

We ask this of you
in the name of the love you have for your Mother,
who is also our Mother
and the first of all the children of God.

Luke 2:22-40.

HANDMAID AND QUEEN

God our Father,
we praise you and give you thanks
for choosing the Virgin Mary
to be the Mother of your Son.

In her, the Word found a servant:
your love makes her a queen.

We pray to you:
Make us follow her as an example
that we might listen to your Word
and put it into practice.

May we then be able to share
the inheritance of eternal joy
that you give us
through your only Son Jesus Christ,
our Savior and our brother.

BLESSED BE THE LORD

Blessed be the Lord,
God and Father of our Lord Jesus Christ.

You have chosen the Virgin Mary
to be the Mother of your Son,
and you wish all ages to proclaim her blessed —
    we pray to you:

Because she learned to love us
by loving her firstborn Son,
help us serve you better
by singing her praises.

Enlarge the hearts of all people
so that they may recognize themselves
as brothers and sisters
and adore her Son, Jesus Christ, our Lord.

Luke 1:38, 42, 48.

PRAYERS

FOR

ALL SEASONS

YOU HAVE CREATED OUR BODIES

Blest are you, O Lord,
through eternity!

Blessed are you, Lord,
for the body of the child
that springs from the heart of its mother
like a rosebud.

Blessed are you, Lord,
for the body of the young maiden
that you have clothed in grace and symmetry
and that is as beautiful as your betrothed,
the Church.

Blessed are you, Lord,
for the bodies of husband and wife
who, in a harmony of flesh,
speak their love to each other.

Blessed are you, Lord,
for the body of the celibate religious,
who spends all the strength of his love
in the service of the Kingdom.

Blessed are you, Lord,
for the body of the old man or woman
whose timeworn face already bears the imprint
of a joy that is more than earthly.

Blessed are you, Lord,
for the disfigured body of one who is dying,
whose moans are not so much from agony
as from pains of being born into heaven.

Blessed are you, Lord,
for the beauty of our human bodies,
especially for the most beautiful of all,
that of your Mother, the Virgin Mary,
"the most blessed of all women,"
illuminated by the light and the splendor of heaven
on the morning of her Assumption.

Blessed are you, Lord,
for your own body!

As a man of sorrows without brightness or beauty,
you were bruised by your sufferings on the cross
yet exalted by your Father in the glory of heaven.
Blessed are you who give us your risen body
as bread from heaven at the feast of the Covenant!

A PRAYER OF RENEWAL

Jesus Christ, risen Lord,
have mercy on us!

Lord Jesus, by your resurrection,
you renew the universe;
you change our death into your life;
    we pray to you:
Jesus Christ, risen Lord, have mercy on us!

Give us kindness wherever you find bitterness,
confidence wherever you find distress,
joy wherever you find sorrow;
    we pray to you:
Jesus Christ, risen Lord, have mercy on us!

Give us humility wherever pride reigns,
pardon wherever offense abides,
grace wherever sin abounds;
    we pray to you:
Jesus Christ, risen Lord, have mercy on us!

Give us love wherever hatred burns,
hope wherever despair is crying,
faith wherever doubt prevails;
    we pray to you:
Jesus Christ, risen Lord, have mercy on us!

Give us a new spirit in our old age,
a new heart to replace a heart of stone,
and the New Covenant in your holy resurrection;
    we pray to you:
Jesus Christ, risen Lord, have mercy on us!

WITH THEM WE PRAY TO YOU

Save us, O Lord, in the name of your love!

Lord Jesus,
you cleansed the leper.
With him we pray to you:
"Lord, if you wish,
heal us!"
Save us, O Lord, in the name of your love!

Lord Jesus,
you cured the centurion's servant.
With him we pray to you:
"Only say the word
and we shall be cured!"
Save us, O Lord, in the name of your love!

Lord Jesus,
you calmed the storm and saved the apostles.
With them we pray to you:
"Lord, save us!
Without you we perish."
Save us, O Lord, in the name of your love!

Lord Jesus,
you walked on the waters.
With Peter we pray to you:
"Lord, save us!
You are the Son of God."
Save us, O Lord, in the name of your love!

Lord Jesus,
you answered the Canaanite woman's request
to cure her daughter.
With her we pray to you:
"Lord, come and help us.
Give us the bread of children!"
Save us, O Lord, in the name of your love!

Lord Jesus,
you raised the daughter of Jairus.
With her father we pray to you:
"Lay your hand upon us,
and we will be saved and live!"
Save us, O Lord, in the name of your love!

Lord Jesus,
you cured the blind Bartimaeus
on the road to Jericho.
With him we pray to you:
"Jesus, Son of David,
have pity on us."
Save us, O Lord, in the name of your love!

Lord Jesus,
you pardoned the good thief on the cross.
With him we pray to you:
"Jesus, remember us
in your Kingdom!"
Save us, O Lord, in the name of your love!

Jesus Christ,
God of all tenderness
and Lord of all mercy,
you who spent your time on earth doing good,
    we pray to you:
Give to each of us our share of joy and happiness,
so that we can, on the road of life,
discover your love constantly,
bless and glorify you,
and arrive at perfect joy,
which is to live near your Father,
with you and the Holy Spirit,
forever and ever.
    Amen!

Matthew 8:1-4, 5-13, 23-27; 14:22-33; 15:21-28
Mark 5:21-43; 10:46 Luke 23:39-43 Acts 10:48.

THE SEVEN MIRACLES OF THE GOSPEL

According to the Gospel of John

Save us, O Lord, in the name of your love!

Lord Jesus,
at Cana in Galilee you changed water into wine.
　We pray to you:
Change to joy the sorrows of our earthly families
to show your glory to the world.
Save us, O Lord, in the name of your love!

Lord Jesus,
at Capernaum you restored to life
the dead son of a royal officer.
　We pray to you:
Revive our faith in the power of your Word
that saves us from death.
Save us, O Lord, in the name of your love!

Lord Jesus,
at the pool of Bethesda you cured a paralytic.
　We pray to you:
Deliver us from the paralysis of sin
and help us to walk with you.
Save us, O Lord, in the name of your love!

Lord Jesus,
in the desert you fed a hungry crowd
with five barley loaves and two fish.
　We pray to you:
Give each person the bread of both earth and heaven
and satisfy our hunger for eternity.
Save us, O Lord, in the name of your love!

Lord Jesus,
you walked on the waters to meet your apostles.
　We pray to you:
Guide the ship of our life
to the shores of eternity.
Save us, O Lord, in the name of your love!

John 2:1-11; 4:46-53; 5:1-8; 6:1-15, 16-21; 9:1-40; 11:1-44.

Lord Jesus,
at Siloam's pool you gave sight to a man born blind.
    We pray to you:
Let your light shine on our world,
pull us out of the darkness of sadness and sin.
Save us, O Lord, in the name of your love!

Lord Jesus,
you called back to life your friend Lazarus
after he had been in his grave four days.
    We pray to you:
On the last day, call us too by our names
and open the door to each grave
that we may, with you and the Holy Spirit,
glorify your Father in eternal joy.
Save us, O Lord, in the name of your love!

THE "OUR FATHER"

According to the Gospel of Luke

One day Jesus was at prayer.
When he had finished,
one of his disciples asked him:
"Lord, teach us to pray
just as John the Baptist taught his disciples."

Jesus said to them:
"Father, hallowed be your name."
    —Your Kingdom come, O Lord!

"Give us each day our daily bread."
    —Your Kingdom come, O Lord!

"Forgive us our sins,
as we ourselves forgive each one
who is in debt to us."
    —Your Kingdom come, O Lord!

"And lead us not into temptation."
    —Your Kingdom come, O Lord!

The "Our Father," *Luke 11:1-4.*

WE ARE THE LEAST OF ALL THE NATIONS

Prayer of the Diaspora

*Have mercy, O Lord,
have mercy on us!*

Blessed are you, O Lord, God of our fathers,
and glorious forever is your holy name!
But do not forget to have pity on your people!

We have sinned by deserting you,
but do not abandon us,
for the sake of Abraham, your friend,
of Isaac, your servant, and Israel, the holy one.

You promised to multiply your people
like the stars of heaven,
like the grains of sand on the shore of the sea.

But now, we are the least of all the nations,
we are despised throughout the whole world,
humiliated because of our sins.

Accept the sacrifice of our contrite hearts,
let it come into your presence today,
treat us gently as you are gentle and merciful.

We will follow you and seek your face.
Deliver us, Lord, by the power of your love
and give glory to your name,
    through Jesus Christ, your Son,
    our Savior and our brother.

Daniel 3:26-43. Diaspora is a Greek word (in Hebrew: *gola*) meaning "disper-
sion" and designating, in the past, the Jews dispersed outside Palestine, and
today the Christian people dispersed all over the world.

WITH THE CHURCH

With the Church in heaven and on earth,
let us glorify the Lord:

Praise to you now and evermore!

With the Virgin Mary, your Mother,
we wish to listen to your Word.
With the patriarchs and prophets,
we wish to announce your Kingdom.

With the apostles and evangelists,
we wish to proclaim the Good News.
With all the disciples who answered your call,
we wish to follow you.

With all the martyrs who offered you their bodies
    in sacrifice,
we wish to give witness to you.
With the saints of all times,
we wish to serve you.

With all those who believe in you,
we offer you the obedience of our faith.
With all those who love you,
we offer you our love.

With all those who seek you in the night,
we wish to walk toward the light.
With all those who are unaware of your name,
we wish to hearn to love you.

With all those whom you invite to the banquet
    of the Kingdom,
invite us also, we beg you.
With all those whom you inscribe in the book of life,
count us among your elect.

With all those who die in you,
we place our hope in your mercy.
With all those who have risen with you,
we sing your praises forever.

KING OF ENDLESS GLORY

Praise to you, Lord Jesus Christ, King of endless glory!

Lord Jesus,
Bright Morning Star,
you announce the eternal day —
    we acclaim you!

Lord Jesus,
Rising Sun, Light of the World,
you shine on those in the shadow of death —
    we acclaim you!

Lord Jesus,
Living Way to the Father,
your footprints lead our path to heaven —
    we acclaim you!

Lord Jesus,
Living Bread from Heaven,
come to satisfy the hunger of the world —
    we acclaim you!

Lord Jesus,
you who are the Good Shepherd,
gather all people into one fold —
    we acclaim you!

Lord Jesus,
Faithful Witness revealing the Father to us,
give strength to the testimony
of those who announce your Word —
    we acclaim you!

Lord Jesus,
True Vine of which we are the branches,
help us to bear much fruit —
    we acclaim you!

Lord Jesus,
Firstborn from the dead,
awaken us when our eternal Day dawns —
    we acclaim you!

*Luke 1:78   John 6:32-58; 10:1-16; 14:6; 15:1-17   Colossians 1:15
Revelation 1:5; 22:16.*

MAY THEY GLORIFY YOU FOR US, O LORD

Praise to you, Lord Jesus Christ, King of endless glory!

May they glorify you for us, O Lord:
the Virgin Mary who bore you,
the crib wherein you lay as an infant,
the angels who sang in the night to you,
the shepherds who came to adore you.

May they glorify you for us, O Lord:
the Magi who came from the East to you,
the star that shone in your sky,
the little children of Bethlehem
who died for you.

May they glorify you for us, O Lord:
the Jordan that flowed with gladness for you,
the precursor John who baptized you,
the apostles and the disciples
who followed your call.

May they glorify you for us, O Lord:
the children who sang "Hosanna" to you,
the tears of your agony,
the chains that bound you,
the thorns that bruised your forehead.

May they glorify you for us, O Lord:
the Calvary whereon your cross was planted,
the bitter death that you suffered,
the new tomb wherein you rested
in the sleep of death.

May they glorify you for us, O Lord:
the morning which saw your awakening,
the angel in white who announced your resurrection,
the holy women who came to embalm you
and met the angels.

May they glorify you for us, O Lord:
the pain and the joy of all people,
the light of our faith,
the strength of our hope,
the peace that comes from your love.

YOU HAVE COME, LORD

Save us, O Lord,
in the name of your love.

You have come, Lord,
to seek out and save what was lost:
Without you, Lord, we are lost.
   Come to save us!

You have come, Lord,
not to call the just, but sinners:
Without you, Lord, we are crushed by our faults.
   Come to save us!

You have come, Lord,
not to abolish the law, but to fulfill it:
Without you, Lord, we cannot live in love.
   Come to save us!

You have come, Lord,
not to be served, but to serve,
and to give your life as a ransom for many:
Without you, Lord, we cannot serve in truth
   our brothers and sisters.
   Come to save us!

You have come, Lord,
to bring fire upon the earth:
Without you, Lord, we die of cold.
Let the fire of your Spirit burn in us!
   Come to save us!

Matthew 5:17; 9:13 Mark 10:45 Luke 12:49; 19:10. This prayer is based on the sentence "I came" (from God) or "The Son of Man came." The primitive Christian community saw in Jesus him "who comes in the name of the Lord" *(Ps 118:26 = Mt 21:9).*

GOD OF TENDERNESS

God of tenderness and pity,
slow to anger and full of love,
we pray to you:
    Deliver us, O Lord.

From all sin and every evil,
from the hardening of our hearts,
from all bad will,
    deliver us, O Lord.

From contempt for your Word,
from refusal of your grace,
from the denial of your call,
    deliver us, O Lord.

From the spirit of jealousy and envy,
from pride and vanity,
from indifference toward our brothers and sisters,
    deliver us, O Lord.

From lukewarmness in your love,
from boredom in your service,
from the sadness of this world,
    deliver us, O Lord.

DELIVER US, LORD

Deliver us, O Lord!

By your coming into the world,
by your birth in Bethlehem,
by your hidden life in Nazareth,
    deliver us, O Lord!

By your baptism in the Jordan,
by your fast in the desert,
by your victory over the devil,
    deliver us, O Lord!

By your preaching of the Kingdom,
by your announcement of the Good News,
by your glorious transfiguration,
    deliver us, O Lord!

By your love for the poor,
by your compassion for their sufferings,
by your tears at the tomb of Lazarus,
    deliver us, O Lord!

By your gift of the Eucharist,
by your agony in the garden of Olives,
by your condemnation before Annas and Caiaphas,
    deliver us, O Lord!

By your carrying of the cross,
by your crucifixion and your agony,
by your death and burial,
    deliver us, O Lord!

By your holy resurrection,
by your glorious ascension,
by the coming of the Holy Spirit,
    deliver us, O Lord!

On the day of judgment
may your mercy be our defense;
your love, our salvation.
    Deliver us, O Lord!

WE BEG YOU, LORD

Save us, O Lord,
without you we are lost!

We beg you, Lord!
See our mistakes: be our truth.
See our straying: be our road.
See our death: be our life.
Save us, O Lord,
without you we are lost!

See our weakness: be our strength.
See our foolishness: be our wisdom.
See our sin: be our pardon.
Save us, O Lord,
without you we are lost!

See our anguish: be our peace.
See our hunger: be our bread.
See our thirst: be our faith.
Save us, O Lord,
without you we are lost!

See our pride: be our humility.
See our darkness: be our light.
See our night: be our star.
Save us, O Lord,
without you we are lost!

Lord Jesus,
you whose name means "Savior,"
we beg you:
For each of us may your name be true.
Save us all, for you are our brother
and our only hope!

PRAYER FOR PEOPLE OF ALL AGES

Have mercy, O Lord,
have mercy on us!

Let us pray for all children:
    Help them to grow in grace and wisdom,
    and in the knowledge of your Son Jesus Christ.

Let us pray for all young men and women:
    Give them a full and happy youth;
    open their hearts to accept
    not only the suffering but also the joy of the world.

Let us pray for all married people
    who have promised before Christ to be faithful
        to each other:
    May the fervor of their love show to the world
    the tenderness of Christ Jesus toward his Church.

Let us pray for all those who are single
    because of the Kingdom of heaven:
    Support them in the joy of their vocation,
    that their lives may show to the world the Kingdom
        that is to come.

Let us pray for all those in the autumn of life:
    Grant them a peaceful and happy old age;
    guide their steps on the road to peace.

Let us pray for all those who have no family and home:
    Show the gentleness of your presence
    to all who live alone
    and have no hope but you.

YOU WERE MOVED TO PITY

Lord, have mercy.

You were moved to pity, Lord,
at the sight of the leper who pleaded with you:
"If you wish, you can cure me."
Heal our brothers and sisters who suffer in their flesh,
and cleanse us all of the leprosy of sin,
    we beg you.
Lord, have mercy.

You were moved to pity, Lord,
at the sight of the crowds weary and abandoned
like sheep without a shepherd.
To those in the prison of fatigue or loneliness,
send someone who will guide them toward hope,
    we beg you.
Lord, have mercy.

You were moved to pity, Lord,
at the sight of the crowds who had nothing to eat.
Give each person the bread of earth
and make each one desire the bread of heaven,
    we beg you.
Lord, have mercy.

You were moved to pity, Lord,
at the sight of two blind men by the roadside
who were crying, "Have pity on us, Son of David!"
Be the light of those who are blind,
and heal the blindness of our hearts,
    we beg you.
Lord, have mercy.

You were moved to pity, Lord,
and your heart beat more quickly
when you saw the tears of the widow of Naim.
To those who are sad today,
repeat the words of old, "Do not cry,"
and heal the sadness of our hearts,
    we beg you.
Lord, have mercy.

Mark 1:41; 6:34; 8:2 Matthew 20:34 Luke 7:13 John 11:35.

You were moved to pity, Lord,
when you saw the tears of Martha and Mary.
You yourself wept at your friend's tomb!
Because you are our life and our resurrection,
open a door of hope to each of our troubles,
    we beg you.
Lord, have mercy.

Lord Jesus,
no sorrow is a stranger to you
and all suffering finds the road to your heart.

Consider the misery of all people:
let not their sufferings be in vain;
let them be joined to the merits of your passion
    and to your resurrection.

SONG OF JUBILATION

Blest are you, O Lord, through eternity!

You have hidden your mystery from the wise and the learned.
    Blest are you, O Lord,
    through eternity!

You have revealed it to mere children.
    Blest are you, O Lord,
    through eternity!

Yes, Father, you have graciously willed it so.
    Blest are you, O Lord,
    through eternity!

The prayer "You Were Moved to Pity" is based on *esplagchnisthe,* a verb used by
the Gospels. Literally it means "He was moved by pity in his bowels" — in his
heart, as we would say today.
Song of Jubilation, *Matthew 11:25-27   Luke 10:21-22.*

YOU WERE BORN FOR US IN TIME

Jesus Christ, risen Lord,
have mercy on us!

You were born for us in time,
so you give us eternal life.
You became poor,
so you make us rich.
You became man,
so we become like God.
    We pray to you:
Jesus Christ, risen Lord, have mercy on us!

You received baptism,
so you wash away our sins.
You fasted in the desert,
so you nourish us.
You were tempted by the devil,
so you give us the victory.
    We pray to you:
Jesus Christ, risen Lord, have mercy on us!

You cured the lepers,
so you purify us.
You gave sight to the blind,
so you enlighten us.
You gave speech to the mute,
so you open our mouths to praise.
    We pray to you:
Jesus Christ, risen Lord, have mercy on us!

You were a prisoner,
so you free us.
You kept silent,
so you instruct us.
You were beaten like a slave,
so you set us free.
    We pray to you:
Jesus Christ, risen Lord, have mercy on us!

You were stripped of your clothes,
so you clothe us with glory.
You were given vinegar to drink,
so you quench our thirst.

You were crowned with thorns,
so you make us kings.
    We pray to you:
Jesus Christ, risen Lord, have mercy on us!

You died on the cross,
so you give us life.
You were humiliated unto death,
so you raise us up to heaven.
You were laid in a tomb,
so you raise us to glory.
    We pray to you:
Jesus Christ, risen Lord, have mercy on us!

Help us, Lord,
to serve you with joy,
to glorify you with humility,
to please you with holiness,
to wait for you with hope,
to love you in the peace of the Holy Spirit.
    We pray to you:
Jesus Christ, risen Lord, have mercy on us!

Gather us into your Kingdom,
where you will fill us with joy,
where you will transform all pain,
where you will wipe away every tear,
on that Day when you will create for eternity
the new heavens and the new earth.
    We pray to you:
Jesus Christ, risen Lord, have mercy on us!

According to the Maronite liturgy.

NO ONE IS A FATHER LIKE YOU, LORD

No one is a father
like you, Lord —
you are a father to us!
May you be blest!

*Blest are you, O Lord,
through eternity!*

You free us from the land of slavery;
you lead us to the kingdom of freedom.
Blest are you, O Lord, through eternity!

As one does for a little child,
you teach us to walk
and hold us in your arms.
Blest are you, O Lord, through eternity!

You lead us with a bridle of kindness;
you guide us with the reins of love.
Blest are you, O Lord, through eternity!

You are like a father to us
who lifts his child to press him close to his cheek,
and you stoop down to us
and give us food.
Blest are you, O Lord, through eternity!

We beg you, Lord:
Because you are our Father,
make us live as your children
so that our entire lives will give you glory,
through Jesus, your Son and our brother.

Hosea 11:1-4.

GLORY TO YOU, FATHER

Glory to you, Father,
through your beloved Son, Jesus Christ,
in the unity of the Holy Spirit!

*Blest are you, Lord,
through eternity!*

May you be blessed, Father,
because you have created me,
and because the heart that you have given me
you held, first of all, in your own hands!
Blest are you, Lord, through eternity!

May you be blessed, Father,
for the soul that you have given me,
because your love has fashioned it
in the image of Jesus, your firstborn Son!
Blest are you, Lord, through eternity!

May you be blessed, Father,
for the body that you have given me,
because you will call it to live eternally
in the glory of your resurrection!
Blest are you, Lord, through eternity!

O Father of Jesus and source of the Spirit,
you who loved me in Christ
even before the world was created,
you who are the source of my whole being
and the root of every good thing that grows in me:
Because I was born in your heart,
let my whole life be only a return to you —
to your heart, where I will finally know
        the peace of my heart.

Ephesians 1:3-6.

THE PARABLE OF THE SOWER

Remember us, O Lord,
in your loving care!

Jesus taught his disciples with parables.
He said to them, "Listen!
One day a farmer went out sowing...."

So that your Word in us, Lord,
does not fall on the roadside
and Satan remove it from our hearts,
    we pray to you.

So that your Word in us, Lord,
does not fall on rocky ground
and we be fickle
at our first temptation,
    we pray to you.

So that your Word in us, Lord,
does not fall among thorns
and the cares of life
and the enticement of riches choke it,
    we pray to you.

So that your Word in us, Lord,
falls on rich and fertile soil
and we yield fruit in abundance,
    we pray to you.

    Lord Jesus,
sower of all the good that is in the world,
place in us the seeds of goodness and justice.
Let our land yield a harvest of human love
and sheaves of joy for eternal life.

Matthew 13:1-23   Mark 4:1-20   Luke 8:4-15.

GIVE YOUR BREAD

O Lord, we pray to you.

Give your bread, Lord, to those who are hungry;
give hunger for yourself to those who have bread;
    for you alone, Lord,
    can satisfy our desire:
    O Lord, we pray to you.

Give your strength to those who are weak;
give humility to those who think themselves strong;
    for you alone, Lord,
    are our strength:
    O Lord, we pray to you.

Give faith to those who are in doubt;
give doubt to those who believe they possess you;
    for you alone, Lord,
    are the truth:
    O Lord, we pray to you.

Give confidence to those who are afraid;
give your fear to those who have too much confidence;
    for you alone, Lord,
    support our hope:
    O Lord, we pray to you.

Give light to those who are searching for you;
preserve in your love those who have found you;
    for you alone, Lord,
    can fulfill our love:
    O Lord, we pray to you.

COME TO ME LIKE A CRY OF JOY

Come, Lord Jesus Christ!

When my life sinks in sadness,
come to me like a cry of joy.
  Come, Lord Jesus Christ!

When my heart is as hard as a rock,
come to me like the dew of springtime.
  Come, Lord Jesus Christ!

When noise invades my haven,
come to me like an oasis of silence.
  Come, Lord Jesus Christ!

When the wind of hate rises within me,
come to me like a kiss of pardon.
  Come, Lord Jesus Christ!

When I am sinking into the darkness of death,
come to me like a child's smile.
  Come, Lord Jesus Christ!

And when the earth encloses me in its arms,
open for me the doors of your mercy.
  Come, Lord Jesus Christ!

YOU HAVE LOVED OUR EARTH, LORD JESUS

May you be blest, O Lord!

You have loved our earth, Lord Jesus,
in the many-colored flowers of the fields
more beautiful than the robe of Solomon,
and in the birds of the sky who worship the Father
by their flapping wings and their joyous chirping —
you said they are the sign of his providence!
　　May you be blest, O Lord!

You have loved our earth, Lord,
as you admired the wedding dress of the bride.
It is beautiful, you said, like the grace
we must have to enter the banquet of the Kingdom.
　　May you be blest, O Lord!

You have loved our earth, Lord,
in the street children playing their pipes and dancing,
and in the little ones brought to you in their mothers' arms.
You loved and even embraced them!
　　May you be blest, O Lord!

You have loved our earth, Lord,
in the sweet-smelling perfume, which fills the house,
and in Mary's hair drying your feet.
You defended her!
　　May you be blest, O Lord!

You have loved our earth, Lord,
in the lightning flash of the storm,
splitting the sky from the east to the west.
Its suddenness, you said, is a sign of the coming Kingdom
that will burst upon the world.
　　May you be blest, O Lord!

You have loved the crimson sky in the evening —
it is the throne of God, you said.
It transfigures the earth,
which you called God's footstool!
　　May you be blest, O Lord!

Matthew 5:35; 6:28-30; 22:11-12; 24:27 Luke 7:31-32; 17:23-24 John 12:3-8.

You have loved our earth, Lord:
When you saw a bird's nest,
you dreamed of a place to lay your head —
which you, O Son of Man, had not!
     May you be blest, O Lord!

You have loved our earth, Lord:
You watched the budding wheat,
hurrying to grow day and night,
so as to ripen as surely as your Kingdom comes.
     May you be blest, O Lord!

You have loved our earth, Lord:
You allowed yourself to be caressed by the evening breeze,
which wanders through the byways of Jerusalem,
as mysterious as the passing of your Spirit.
     May you be blest, O Lord!

You have loved our earth, Lord:
When you foresaw the morning star
gleaming through the rosy light of dawn,
you thought of your own mystery —
you who are for all who seek you
the shining star of eternal morning!
     May you be blest, O Lord!

We beg you, Lord:
Because you have loved our earth,
which has become yours by your birth in Bethlehem,
make us, too, by loving it,
learn to prefer heaven to it
until the day when you will create for eternity
the new heavens and the new earth.

Matthew 8:20 Mark 4:26-29 John 3:8 Revelation 22:16.

YOU CHOOSE THE WEAK

The powerful of the world are held in esteem,
but it is the weak whom you have chosen.
     We bless you:
Blest are you, O Lord, through eternity!

The learned people of the world are proud,
but it is the simple whom you embrace.
     We bless you:
Blest are you, O Lord, through eternity!

Those who claim a noble birth are proud,
but it is those who are despised, those with no name,
whom you have chosen as your brothers and sisters.
     We bless you:
Blest are you, O Lord, through eternity!

The wisdom of the world is tempting,
but it is the folly of the cross that you prefer.
     We bless you:
Blest are you, O Lord, through eternity!

     Lord Jesus,
you who save us through your cross of light,
which is a scandal and a folly for pagans,
but a power of salvation for those who believe,
     we implore you:
Give us that supreme wisdom
to accept our weakness,
so as to be saved only by the power of your love,
you who are the God of the humble
and the friend of the poor.

1 Corinthians 1:18-31.

PRAYER OF THE BEATITUDES

Blest are those who are invited to the banquet of the Kingdom.

Lord Jesus, you said,
"Blest are the poor in spirit;
the reign of God is theirs."
Give us the spirit of poverty and humility.

Lord Jesus, you said,
"Blest too are the sorrowing;
they shall be consoled."
Teach us to share the tears of our brothers and sisters.

Lord Jesus, you said,
"Blest are the lowly;
they shall inherit the land."
Give us a heart as lowly and humble as yours.

Lord Jesus, you said,
"Blest are they who hunger and thirst for holiness;
they shall have their fill."
Give us souls athirst for justice and love.

Lord Jesus, you said,
"Blest are they who show mercy;
mercy shall be theirs."
Open our hearts with love for our brothers and sisters.

Lord Jesus, you said,
"Blest are the single-hearted,
for they shall see God."
Enlighten our eyes with your splendor.

Lord Jesus, you said,
"Blest too are the peacemakers;
they shall be called children of God."
Make us channels of peace and joy.

Lord Jesus, you said,
"Blest are those persecuted for righteousness' sake;
the reign of God is theirs."
Make us strong in suffering for the Kingdom.

Matthew 5:3-12.

MAY IT RISE

Let the light of your face
shine upon us!

May the kindness of your face
   rise above the hardness of our hearts.
May the humility of your heart
   rise above the foolishness of our pride.
Let the light of your face shine upon us!

May the joy of your mercy
   rise above the sadness of our sins.
May the splendor of your eternal Day
   rise above the sleep of our death.
Let the light of your face shine upon us!

May the freedom of the children of God
   rise above our slavery.
May the peace of your love
   rise above our anguish.
Let the light of your face shine upon us!

May the dawn of your resurrection
   rise above the night of our world.
May the glory of God
   rise within the heart of each person.
Let the light of your face shine upon us!

"I AM"

Remember us, O Lord,
in your Kingdom.

Lord Jesus, you said,
"I am the bread of life."
Satisfy our hunger for eternity,
    we pray to you.

Lord Jesus, you said,
"I am the light of the world."
Light up our darkness with your splendor,
    we pray to you.

Lord Jesus, you said,
"I am the gate of the sheepfold."
Lead us to your Kingdom,
    we pray to you.

Lord Jesus, you said,
"I am the good shepherd."
Gather us into your fold,
    we pray to you.

Lord Jesus, you said,
"I am the resurrection and the life."
Awaken us from the sleep of death,
    we pray to you.

Lord Jesus, you said,
"I am the way, the truth, and the life."
Show us the face of your Father,
    we pray to you.

Lord Jesus, you said,
"I am the true vine."
Help us to bear fruit in your love,
    we pray to you.

John 6:35; 8:12; 10:7; 11:25; 14:6; 15:1. The prayer "I Am" is based on the *Ego eimi* sentences of the Gospel of John. Jesus affirms that he is for the messianic people what Yahve ("I am who am." *Exodus 3:14)* was for the people of the Exodus.

GOD OF OUR CHILDHOOD

Remember us, O Lord,
in your loving care.

God of our childhood,
you whose name we have learned
in the smiles of our father and mother,
    we beg you:
Preserve in us a childlike spirit
so that we can enter your Kingdom.

God of our adolescence,
you who have created the eagerness of youth,
who know its desires and its follies,
    we beg you:
Preserve the flower of hope in our hearts;
be always the God of the joy of our youth.

God of our maturity,
you who call us
to make fruitful the gifts you have put in us,
    we beg you:
Help each of us to become that perfect Man
who realizes the fullness of Christ.

God of our old age,
at the time when the spirit loses its ardor,
when the body becomes feeble,
    we beg you:
Remain close to us when the night comes.
You are our God for all eternity.

Ephesians 4:13.

HOLY ARE YOUR WAYS!

Holy, holy, holy is the Lord,
for eternal is his love!

It is written in the psalm:
"O God, holy are your ways!"

Holy is the journey of my life toward you
and the way from my captivity to your freedom.
> Holy, holy is the Lord,
> for eternal is his love!

Holy is the joy that stirs me with enthusiasm
and makes me run swiftly on your road.
> Holy, holy is the Lord,
> for eternal is his love!

Holy are the troubles that crush me with weariness
and that slow down my progress.
> Holy, holy is the Lord,
> for eternal is his love!

Holy are the meetings with all my friends
who journey with me toward your dwelling.
> Holy, holy is the Lord,
> for eternal is his love!

Holy, too, is the death that awaits me at the road's end,
for then I will be very close to your home!
> Holy, holy is the Lord,
> for eternal is his love!

Help me to understand, Lord,
that what counts is not the road traveled,
but simply putting my hand in yours
and journeying side by side with you, Lord Jesus —
O you who are the joy of my journey
and also the repose in the Father's home!
> Holy, holy is the Lord,
> for eternal is his love!

Psalm 77:14 Hebrews 13:14.

WATCH OVER YOUR CHURCH

O Lord, we pray to you.

Watch over your Church;
    make it perfect in your love.
O Lord, we pray to you.

Gather all the baptized
    into the unity of the faith.
O Lord, we pray to you.

Lead all people
    to the light of the Gospel.
O Lord, we pray to you.

Give to all people
    peace with justice.
O Lord, we pray to you.

To those who remember the poor
    give everlasting reward.
O Lord, we pray to you.

Strengthen all our brothers and sisters
    in the service of the Kingdom.
O Lord, we pray to you.

Lift our souls
    toward the desires of heaven.
O Lord, we pray to you.

Give to our deceased brothers and sisters
    life in eternal light.
O Lord, we pray to you.

AN ANGEL SPOKE THROUGH MY DARKNESS

Open my eyes, O Jesus, Lord!

An angel spoke through my darkness:
"Clothe your soul with light
and you will find the day,
    Christ Jesus."
Open my eyes, O Jesus, Lord!

An angel spoke through my pain:
"Clothe your soul with patience
and you will find peace,
    Christ Jesus."
Open my eyes, O Jesus, Lord!

An angel spoke through my agony:
"Clothe your soul with confidence
and you will find rest,
    Christ Jesus."
Open my eyes, O Jesus, Lord!

An angel spoke through my dying:
"Clothe your soul in life
and you will find eternity,
    Christ Jesus."
Open my eyes, O Jesus, Lord!

LIFE OF MY LIFE

My Lord and my God!

Life of my life,
keep my heart pure
and make your dwelling there!
    My Lord and my God!

Light of my light,
disperse my darkness
so that I can see you!
    My Lord and my God!

Truth beyond truth,
drive falsehood from me
so that my life will be transparent.
    My Lord and my God!

Joy of my joy,
preserve me from sadness
so that your smile will blossom on my lips.
    My Lord and my God!

And when evening comes,
let the dawn of eternal life
rise for me!
    My Lord and my God!

JESUS, WORD OF THE FATHER

Praise to you, O Lord!
or *Save us, O Lord, in the name of your love!*

Jesus, Word of the Father,	*Jn 1:1*
Jesus, everlasting Wisdom,	*1 Cor 1:24*
Jesus, Son of God.	*Rom 1:4*
Jesus, Son of Man,	
Jesus, Son of David,	
Jesus, Son of Abraham.	*Mt 1:1*
Jesus, Son of Mary,	
Jesus, Son of Joseph,	*Mt 1:16*
Jesus, the Carpenter.	*Mk 6:3*
Jesus, the Messiah,	*Jn 1:41; 4:25*
Jesus, the Emmanuel,	*Mt 1:23*
Jesus, "the One who comes in the name of the Lord."	*Mk 11:9; Lk 13:35*
Jesus, the light of the world,	*Jn 8:12*
Jesus, sun of justice,	*Mal 4:2*
Jesus, morning star.	*Rv 22:16*
Jesus, living path to the Father,	*Heb 10:19*
Jesus, our life,	
Jesus, our truth.	*Jn 14:6*
Jesus, the Holy and Just,	*Acts 13:14*
Jesus, the Advocate,	*1 Jn 2:1*
Jesus, the just Judge.	*2 Tm 4:6-8*
Jesus, the new Adam,	*1 Cor 15:45*
Jesus, our life,	*Jn 1:4*
Jesus, our resurrection.	*Jn 11:25*
Jesus, priest of the New Covenant,	*Heb 8:6*
Jesus, merciful and faithful priest,	*Heb 2:17*
Jesus, mediator between God and man.	*1 Tm 2:5*
Jesus, the good shepherd,	*Jn 10:11*
Jesus, gate of the sheepfold,	*Jn 10:7*
Jesus, Lamb of God.	*Jn 1:29*

Jesus, prophet risen from among us,	*Lk 7:16*
Jesus, our Master,	*Mk 9:5*
Jesus, meek and humble of heart.	*Mt 11:29*
Jesus, our peace,	*Eph 2:14*
Jesus, our Redeemer,	*1 Cor 1:30*
Jesus, ransom for our sins.	*1 Jn 4:10; Mk 10:45*
Jesus, the Savior,	*Mt 1:21*
Jesus, Prince of life,	*Acts 3:15*
Jesus, Head of our faith.	*Heb 12:2*
Jesus, light of life,	*Jn 8:12*
Jesus, bread of heaven,	*Jn 6:35*
Jesus, living water springing to eternal life.	*Jn 4:10*
Jesus, our justice,	
Jesus, our holiness,	
Jesus, our redemption.	*1 Cor 1:30*
Jesus, beloved Son,	*Eph 1:6*
Jesus, firstborn of many brothers and sisters,	*Rom 8:29*
Jesus, our Amen to the glory of the Father.	*2 Cor 2:19*
Jesus, cornerstone of the Church,	*Acts 4:11*
Jesus, rock of Israel,	*1 Cor 10:4*
Jesus, spouse of the messianic community.	*2 Cor 11:2*
Jesus, resurrected Lord,	*Rom 10:9*
Jesus, Savior of the world,	*1 Jn 4:14; Jn 4:42*
Jesus, king of justice and peace.	*Mt 21:5; Heb 7:2*
Jesus, Wonderful Counselor,	
Jesus, Divine Hero,	
Jesus, Prince of peace.	*Is 9:6*
Jesus, faithful Witness,	*Rv 1:5*
Jesus, Firstborn from among the dead,	*Col 1:18*
Jesus, Prince of the kings of the earth.	*Rv 1:5*
Jesus, Image of the invisible God,	*Col 1:15*
Jesus, Splendor of his glory,	*Heb 1:3*
Jesus, Son and Heir.	*Heb 1:2*

Jesus, true Vine of which we are the branches,   *Jn 15:1*
Jesus, Firstborn of all creatures,   *Col 1:15*
Jesus, Head of the Body, your Church.   *Col 1:18*

Jesus, the First and the Last, the Living One,   *Rv 1:17*
Jesus, the Alpha and the Omega,   *Rv 1:8; 21:6*
Jesus, the Beginning and the End.   *Rv 22:13*

JESUS, THE NEW COVENANT

You are my love, O Lord,
you are my joy!

Jesus, the New Covenant,
Jesus, our peace,
pardon for our sins.

Jesus, the Holy and Just One,
Jesus, the Messiah,
Jesus, the Emmanuel.

Jesus, the road to the Father,
Jesus, our life
and our truth.

Jesus, light of the world,
Sun of justice,
Morning Star.

Jesus, meek and humble Messiah,
Shepherd of Israel,
and gate of the sheepfold.

Jesus, eternal Word,
and the Word made flesh,
Wisdom of the Most High.

Jesus, Son of Mary,
Jesus, the Savior,
Jesus, Son of God.

SONG OF CREATION

Blest are you, O Lord,
through eternity!

For you, O Lord of eternity,
    creation celebrates;
of the brightness of your infinite splendor
    its beauty sings.
For you the birds
    lift their voices in the trees;
you are he whom their flapping wings
    try to adore.
Blest are you, O Lord, through eternity!

For you the sheep
    romp in the fields
and the lambs dance on their feet
    among the scarlet poppies.
For you the fish glide in the water;
    before your face they jump for joy.
For you the clouds leap across the heavens,
    and the wind's murmur travels the hills.
Blest are you, O Lord, through eternity!

You are he who hears the chick speak in its shell
    and fills it with the breath of life.
You alone give it strength to break its egg and cry
    so it can call its mother.
You are he who created the rivers in the sky
    and the waves of rain upon the mountains.
Your sun sends its rays to nourish the prairie
    and bleach the desert rocks.
Blest are you, O Lord, through eternity!

You are he who opens the doors
    for the shades of night,
who strokes the horizon
    with the fingers of dawn.
Yours is the sun whose heat leaps up in the east,
    a fountain of life.
You are he who clothes the earth with your beauty,
    yours is the lightning that splits the clouds.
Blest are you, O Lord, through eternity!

You are he who directs the dance of the seasons
   and makes the jonquils bloom in the meadows.
At the kiss of your warmth
   the grain of the wheat in the ground feels comfort.
You are he who clothes the flowers of the field
   with their colorful garb.
Before your face they open their mouths
   to drink their fullness of warmth.
Blest are you, O Lord, through eternity!

You are he who gives unto a man the seed
   to conceive a child
   in the womb of its mother;
you are he who comforts him so he does not cry,
   who opens his mouth,
   and who teaches him speech.
You are he who instills in the heart of a husband
   his love for his wife,
and in a father his laugh when he sees his own self
   in the eyes of his child.
Blest are you, O Lord, through eternity!

Wonderful are your works, O Lord:
   You created the world to show us your love!
You give food to each of us
   and you measure the length of our days.
You send forth your Spirit and all are created,
   and the face of the earth you renew.
You, God, are alone — none other like you!
   All creation takes life from your beauty.
And you live in my heart —
   it is there that I know you!
Blest are you, O Lord, through eternity!

To all who admire your beauty, O Lord,
in the work of your hands,
some day let your face shine forth in its splendor
with the sweetness of your love as Father
   in the face of Jesus your Son,
   the firstborn of all creatures!

This text was inspired (partially) by the sapiential literature of Egypt, particularly by a poem of Akhenaton (fourteenth century before Jesus Christ). That
poem itself inspired *Psalm 104* of the Bible.

WE GIVE YOU THANKS

Prayer of the Didache

We thank you, Father,
for the holy vine of David, your servant,
which you have revealed through Jesus, your Son.
    Praise to you now and evermore!

We thank you, Father,
for the life and the knowledge
that you have revealed through Jesus, your Son.
    Praise to you now and evermore!

Just as this bread that we break
    was once distributed on a hillside
and its fragments gathered so as not to lose any,
so let your Church be gathered
from the farthest parts of the earth into your Kingdom.
    Praise to you now and evermore!

Because yours are the glory and the power forever.
    Praise to you now and evermore!

We thank you, holy Father,
for your holy name that dwells in our hearts.
    Praise to you now and evermore!

For the knowledge, the faith, and the immortality
that you have revealed to us through Jesus, your Son.
    Praise to you now and evermore!

It is you, all-powerful Master, who created the universe
    in praise of your name.
    Praise to you now and evermore!

You give food and drink to the children of men;
but to us you give the grace of a spiritual food,
of a drink for eternal life through Jesus, your Son.
    Praise to you now and evermore!

Above all, we thank you for your power.
    Praise to you now and evermore!

Remember, Lord, your Church,
to deliver it from every evil,
and to make it perfect in your love.
        Praise to you now and evermore!

Gather together from the four winds
this santified Church
into the kingdom that you have prepared.
        Praise to you now and evermore!

Come, Lord, and let this world pass!   —*Amen.*
Hosanna to the house of David!   —*Amen.*
Let him who is holy come!   —*Amen.*
Let him who is not, repent!   —*Amen.*
Marana tha (Come, Lord)!   —*Amen.*

THE GREAT PRAYER
of
Clement of Rome

Praise to you, O Lord!

May the Creator of the universe
keep intact the number of his elect in the whole world,
    through Jesus Christ, your beloved Son.
    Praise to you, O Lord!

Through him you have called us from the darkness
    into the light,
from ignorance to the full knowledge of your glory,
to the hope of your name, source of all creation.
    Praise to you, O Lord!

You have opened the eyes of our hearts
    so that they recognize you,
you, the only Most High in the highest heavens,
the Holy One who dwells among the saints.
    Praise to you, O Lord!

You humble the insolence of the proud;
you defeat the plans of nations;
you exalt the humble; you humble the powerful.
    Praise to you, O Lord!

You enrich and you make poor;
you give death; you save and give life,
unique Benefactor of spirits and the God of all creation.
    Praise to you, O Lord!

You contemplate the abyss;
you survey the works of humans,
you, the help of those who are in danger,
their Savior in despair,
Creator and guardian of every spirit!
    Praise to you, O Lord!

You multiply the peoples of the earth,
and, from among them all, you choose those who love you,
through Jesus Christ, your beloved Son;
through him you have instructed, sanctified, and glorified us.
    Praise to you, O Lord!

We pray to you, O Master,
that you be our help and our support.
Lord, listen to us!

The afflicted — save them;
the lowly — have pity on them.
Lord, listen to us!

The fallen — lift them up;
the needy — give yourself to them.
Lord, listen to us!

The sick — cure them;
your people who have strayed — bring them home.
Lord, listen to us!

Fill those who are hungry;
free those who are prisoners.
Lord, listen to us!

Strengthen those who are feeble;
console those who are fearful.
Lord, listen to us!

May all peoples recognize that you alone are God,
that Jesus Christ is your Son,
that we are your people and the sheep of your pasture.
Lord, listen to us!

Clement of Rome, "Letter to the Corinthians" (about 95-96).

LET US CALL UPON GOD WITH FAITH

Let us call with faith upon God our Father,
through Jesus Christ, his beloved Son,
in the Holy Spirit, who inspires our prayer:
  Remember us, O Lord,
  in your loving care!

For the spotless Church of Jesus Christ,
that it may show forth unto the world
    the glory of the Lord,
let us ask for the riches of divine goodness.
Remember us, O Lord, in your loving care!

For those who faithfully dispense
    the word of truth,
for those who exercise authority
    in the service of their brothers and sisters,
let us ask for the infinite wisdom of the Word of God.
Remember us, O Lord, in your loving care!

For those who live in celibacy
    for the sake of the Kingdom of heaven,
for those who labor and spend themselves
    in spiritual works,
let us call upon him who bestows the gifts of the Spirit.
Remember us, O Lord, in your loving care!

For those who direct the people,
that they may govern according to right and justice,
let us call upon the King of kings and Master of nations.
Remember us, O Lord, in your loving care!

For those who are beginning to know
    the name of the Lord Jesus
and ardently desire divine mercy,
let us call upon him who is the way, the truth, and the life.
Remember us, O Lord, in your loving care!

For those held captive
    by human weakness and frailty,
    by the spirit of envy and hatred,
    by the many errors of the world,
let us implore the mercy of our Redeemer.
Remember us, O Lord, in your loving care!

For those who suffer
    in their flesh or their spirit,
those oppressed, slandered, or hopeless,
let us call upon the Lord who is close to despondent hearts.
Remember us, O Lord, in your loving care!

For those who have been victims of error or lies,
those who do not know the light of the Gospel,
    for those who despise it,
let us call upon the Lord of truth.
Remember us, O Lord, in your loving care!

For those whose love comes to the aid of the poor,
those who share their bread
    with their less fortunate brothers and sisters,
let us pray to the Lord, the friend of the poor.
Remember us, O Lord, in your loving care!

For all of us gathered here,
that we may receive our daily bread
    and pardon for our sins,
let us call upon our Father in heaven.
Remember us, O Lord, in your loving care!

For our brothers and sisters who have left this world,
that they enjoy eternal light and peace,
let us pray to Jesus Christ, firstborn from the dead.
Remember us, O Lord, in your loving care!

Based on the prayer which Pope Gelasius (492-496) "prescribed for singing by
the universal Church."

THE FIRSTBORN OF MANY

Lord Jesus,
you came among us,
the firstborn of many brothers and sisters.

You have walked upon our earth;
you have eaten our bread;
your eyes have seen our light;
your smile has lit up our faces;
and our tears have dampened your eyes.
　　We pray to you:

Because you became like us
in all things except sin,
make us like you in grace.

Send us your Holy Spirit
that he may fashion us for eternity.
May your Father recognize your voice in our prayer.
May he say to each one of us:
"This is my Son, my beloved.
My favor rests on him!"

Listen to us, Lord:
We are your Church;
we are your Body, and flesh of your flesh.
You are our God and our brother,
forever and ever.
　　Amen!

Matthew 3:17 Romans 8:29 Hebrews 4:15.

TO SAVE US

God our Father,
who send your Son Jesus Christ into the world
not to judge it but to save it,
    listen to our prayer:

By giving us your Son, you offer each of us
your light for our darkness,
your joy for our sadness,
your bread to nourish our life,
and your life to overcome our death.

Open our hearts to your word and your grace
so that we may recognize
in you, our Father who calls us by our name,
in your Son, our Savior and brother,
in your Spirit, the love that unites us.

And while our lips sing your praise,
bring our hearts close to you,
through Jesus Christ, our Lord.
    Amen.

John 12:47.

SOURCE OF ALL JOY

God our Father, source of all joy,
        we pray to you:

Help us to understand
that our heaven begins today
when we seek and learn to love you
in the service of our brothers and sisters.

Reveal also your Church to all people.
Let it be the land of their liberty;
let their faces shine
        with the joy of your Son.

FIRE ON THE EARTH

For a long time I have given up
trying to revive the ashes of my dreams.
My hearth is dead.

But you, Lord — did you not come
to bring fire on the earth?

Burn my heart
with the flame of your heart,
you who alone can change
the ashes of my dreams
into a fire of love.

Luke 12:49.

YOUR LOVE FILLS THE EARTH

God our Father, you who tell us
that your love fills the earth
and that your tenderness is for each person
that of a father for his children,
    we pray to you:

Make your light shine in our hearts
so that we can recognize
that your Word is true,
and that your love rests upon each of us
when you give us your only Son, Jesus Christ.

Give us the grace, Lord,
to look for you in the love of our brothers and sisters,
to discover your name in their faces,
to meet you in the heart of our life,
and to reveal to all people
that you wish to fill them with your joy and peace,

in Christ Jesus, your Son,
our Savior and our brother.
    Amen.

Psalm 33:5; 103:13.

"I DESPISE YOUR FEASTS"

Lord God,
by the mouth of your prophet Amos you tell us:
"I hate and despise your feasts;
I want none of your holocausts.
Let me have no more of the din of your chanting,
no more of your strumming on harps.
But let justice flow like water,
and righteousness like an unfailing stream."

Because you judge us by our hearts
and not by our songs,
because you judge us by the depth of our love
and not by the weight of our offerings,
        we beg you:

Let our feast be to come to the aid
        of the poor and the oppressed,
our song be to practice justice,
and our holocaust be the offering
        of a contrite and humble heart.

Then, when our lips sing to you,
our hearts will be celebrating a feast
and you will love our song.

Amos 5:21-24.

PRAYER OF THE LONELY

Lord, listen to me.
Even surrounded by my friends,
I sometimes feel loneliness that enters my heart
like the sorrow of a winter night.

So I beg you:
Give me as my family
all the angels and the saints
who live in your presence.
Let them speak to me about you,
those who know how much you love us.

Then, with a happy heart,
I will go to find my brothers and sisters to tell them
that you are expecting all of us in your home
for the eternal celebration.

ONE UPON WHOM YOU CAST YOUR EYES

Heaven is your throne, Lord,
and the earth is your footstool.
Every wonderful thing that we can offer you
    for a dwelling
your hand has given us.

But the one upon whom you cast your eyes
is the one who is poor and has a contrite heart,
the one who reveres your word.

Lord, fill our hearts with poverty
    so that they may become
a worthy dwelling place for your glory.

Ephesians 2:19 Isaiah 66:1.

LIKE CHILDREN

Like children playing on the beach,
we have built houses of sand.
The wave of time has come
and the laughter of the tides has submerged
        everything.

But we know, Lord,
that, if our earthly home is destroyed,
you will build us an eternal home
        near you in heaven.

Give us the strength to leave our earthly
        dwellings
and our games in the sand.
Direct our boats
toward the shores of eternity.

TO EACH OF US OUR SHARE OF JOY AND HAPPINESS

Lord Jesus,
God of all tenderness
and of all mercy,
you who spent your time on earth doing good,
        we pray to you:
Give to each of us our share of joy and happiness,
so that we can, on our road of life,
discover your love constantly,
bless and glorify you,
and arrive at perfect joy,
which is to live near your Father,
with you and the Holy Spirit,
forever and ever.
        Amen!

2 Corinthians 5:1 Acts 10:38.

USELESS SERVANTS

For your love, Lord, we labor all day long;
for your Kingdom, we struggle all our lives.

And now you tell us:
"You are useless servants."

We are delighted, Lord,
to be such servants.
For we can now implore you:
Give us your Kingdom for nothing,
that is, simply because you love us,
and because Jesus Christ is our brother.

YOU WHO MEASURE THE OCEANS

You, Lord, who measure the oceans in the hollow
    of your hand,
who calculate the dimensions of the heavens
    with your extended fingers,
you who weigh the mountains in scales,
and the hills in a balance,

You before whom the nations
are like a drop of water on the rim of a pail,
like a grain of dust on the scales —
You, the wonderful and magnificent Lord,
    we beg you:

Remember that we are dust
and that from the dust you formed
    the body of your Son Jesus,
our Savior and our brother forever.

Luke 17:10   Isaiah 40:12-15.

MY WORDS WITHER AWAY

Lord of glory and of pity,
my words wither away in singing of your beauty;
my music breaks apart before your grandeur;
and to reecho your love,
I find myself without melody.

Accept my weariness as praise;
take my silence
       as a song of joy.

WONDERFUL IS OUR LIFE

The whole day long the bee has buzzed with joy;
the flower has sung its song with color;
the leaf of the tree has trembled with pleasure.

Your creation is wonderful, Lord!

More wonderful still is our life,
because you fill it with your presence
and your smile pours over our faces
     with your beauty.

PRAYER FOR MISSIONARIES

With the apostle Paul, we pray, Lord,
for all engaged in missionary labor.

May they serve the Lord with complete humility
    in the midst of their trials.
May their own lives seem less important in their sight
than the mission they have received from the Lord Jesus:
to bear witness to the Good News of God's graciousness.

May they never recoil from the necessity
of announcing the entire design of God.
May they carefully watch over the flock
that the Holy Spirit has entrusted to their care.

May they not covet anyone's money.
May the work of their hands provide
for their needs and for those of the poor.

May they remember the words of Jesus:
"There is more happiness in giving
than receiving."

May they, even today, receive
the reward promised to missionaries:
the daily, ever increasing joy
    of laboring for the sake of your Kingdom.

Paul's farewell address to the elders of the Church of Ephesus, *Acts 20:18-35.*

FOR THE AUTHORITIES OF THE CHURCH

We pray, God our Father,
for those who hold authority in the Church:

May they shepherd the flock of God
    that is entrusted to them.
May they watch over it not merely as a duty,
    but gladly, because God wants it;
not for love of sordid gain,
    but with devotion of heart;
not acting as dictators over their brothers and sisters,
    but as examples that the whole flock can follow.

And when Christ, the chief Shepherd, returns,
may they receive the reward promised
    to the sheep that you love.

THE HARVEST IS ABUNDANT

"The harvest is abundant,
but the laborers are few."
    We ask you, Lord:
Send laborers to your harvest!

May they announce the Kingdom
and cure the sick.

As they travel, may they take along
neither the power of money
nor the strength of brute force,
but only your peace.

May their entire lives proclaim:
"The Kingdom of God is very near to you!"

1 Peter 5:1-5 Luke 9:1-5; 10:1-12.

AS A DOE

As a doe longs for running water,
so my soul longs for you, my God!

My soul thirsts for God, the living God:
When shall I go to see your face,
    O Father of Jesus,
     my Christ and my brother,
     and source of the Spirit,
     love in my heart!

MY SOUL THIRSTS FOR YOU

God — it is you, my God — I search for you!
My soul thirsts for you
like a parched, weary, waterless land!

For me, your love, Lord,
is better than life.

I sing for joy in the shadow of your wings;
my soul clings close to you.

Be my help, O my God,
in your Son Jesus Christ.

Psalms 42, 63.

AS A CHILD IN ITS MOTHER'S ARMS

Lord, when I pray,
too often I get so taken up with words
that I no longer hear your voice.

But today I want to keep my soul at peace before you
as a child in its mother's arms.

Let my words become silence,
and let my silence become prayer.

YOU HAVE LAID YOUR HAND ON ME

Lord, you have laid your hand on me;
Lord, you have called me by name.
    I beg you:
Keep me in the palm of your hand;
do not forget my name;
call me to you.

BE PERFECT

Our Father in heaven,
your Son Jesus tells us,
"Be perfect
as your heavenly Father is perfect."

Because he asks the impossible of us,
    we beg you:
Accept, in our place, the offering of
    your beloved Son —
he alone is as perfect as you.

Psalm 131   Psalm 139:5   Matthew 5:48.

A FAMINE OF THE WORD

Thus speaks the Lord:
"See what days are coming
when I will bring famine on the country,
a famine not of bread, a drought not of water,
but of hearing the Word of the Lord."

See, Lord God, our distress:
We have eaten the bitter bread of our illusions
      without being satisfied.
And we have drunk water from our old wells
      without quenching our thirst.

But now we want no more
      than your Word alone,
      your Son Jesus Christ,
      bread of eternal life!

YOUR WORD, LORD

Your Word, Lord — is it not in the heavens?
So we must say:
"Who will go up to heaven for us
and bring it down to us,
so that we may hear it
and keep it?"

Your Word, Lord — is it not beyond the seas?
So we must say:
"Who will cross the seas for us
and bring it back for us,
so that we may hear it
and keep it?"

Your Word, Lord, is very near to us;
it is your Son Jesus Christ,
living in our hearts.

Amos 8:11 Deuteronomy 30:11-14.

LIKE THE PATRIARCH ENOCH

Grant us the same grace, O Lord,
that you gave to the patriarch Enoch.
It is written in the Holy Book:
"Enoch walked with God."

Day after day,
and during every moment of each day,
allow us to place our hands in yours
and walk with you.

LIKE ABRAHAM

Like Abraham,
I have left everything, Lord,
and no longer have a dwelling place.

Now, Lord, give me your mercy
for a dwelling place.

FOR I AM ALONE

Prayer of Esther

O my Lord, our God, no one is like you!
Come to my aid, for I am alone;
I have no recourse but you.
Listen to the voice of the hopeless!
Deliver us from evil;
free us from all anguish.

Save us
through your Son Jesus Christ.

Genesis 5:24; 12:1-4 Esther 4:17(Vg).

YOU HAVE SEDUCED ME, LORD

You have seduced me, Lord,
and I have let myself be seduced.
You have overpowered me,
for you were the stronger.

Continue, Lord, I beg you,
to hold my heart in your hand.
Let me see in all human love
 a spark of your love,
and in all the beauty of the earth
 the reflection of your splendor.

IN THE POTTER'S HAND

Like clay in the hands of the potter,
so are we in your hands, Lord.

Reveal to us the richness of your glory:
We are vases filled with your mercy.

LIKE THE MORNING MIST

Look, Lord, at our weakness.

Our love for you is like the morning mist
that dissolves at the first ray of sunlight,
like the dew at dawn
that is dried up by the first breath of wind.

Give us, Lord, give us
a love simple and pure,
a love that the heat of evil cannot dry up,
that the breath of doubt cannot touch,
a love simple and pure
like the love of a child for its father.

Jeremiah 20:7; 18:1-12 Romans 9:23 Hosea 6:4.

MAY YOU BE BLESSED, LORD

May you be blessed, Lord, because you are God:
    the help of the oppressed,
    the support of the weak,
    the refuge of the forsaken,
    the savior of the despairing.
May you be blessed, Lord, because you are our God!

GO, EAT YOUR BREAD WITH JOY

    God our Father,
you have said to each of us:
"Go, eat your bread with joy!"
    We pray to you:

Give each of us, along with our daily bread,
our share of joy and happiness,
so that we may recognize you as God
and may love you as Father.

HAPPY THE POOR

Lord Jesus, you love the poor,
and you declare them "happy,"
for theirs is the Kingdom of heaven.
    We pray:

Give us hearts so poor
that they may be enriched
    by your love.

We ask this of you
in the name of your Son Jesus,
who, though he was rich,
    made himself poor
to enrich us by his poverty.

Judith 9:11   Ecclesiastes 9:7   Matthew 5:3   2 Corinthians 8:9.

MAY YOUR KINDNESS, O LORD

"May your kindness, O Lord, be upon us
who have put our hope in you."

To those who have little hope,
        you give little.

To those who have much hope,
        you give much.

To us who dare to hope for everything,
give, O Lord, all your love,
you who have offered us everything
        in your Son Jesus Christ.

And if our hearts are too small
to receive your royal generosity,
let your merciful hand, we pray,
        open them to your love.

YOUR PATHS ARE LOVE AND TRUTH

        God our Father,
your Holy Spirit moves us to pray in the psalm:
"All of God's paths are love and truth."

Help us to understand, O Lord,
that these words are true!

This joy that overwhelms us,
this grief that consumes us,
this despair that lies in wait for us
        like a savage beast at the bend
        in a path through undergrowth,
and even this dull day,
which covers us like a mantle of boredom,
all these are the way by which
        your love and fidelity come to us.

Psalm 33:22   Romans 8:32   Psalm 25:10.

"I AM GOING TO PREPARE A PLACE FOR YOU"

That empty place in heaven
that you have prepared for me —
remember it always, Lord!

O do not forget me, my God and my love!
See how I labor on the way!

Send me your holy angels
that I may not get lost on the road!

And all my friends who are already at home with you,
quickly let them run to meet me
    that I may not be late
for the eternal celebration of your mercy!

GOD OUR FATHER

God our Father,
you who are Love,
you who give to this Love
the face of a man in your Son Jesus Christ,
    we pray:

Help us never to doubt your tenderness,
to entrust ourselves always to your mercy,
and to walk humbly with your Son,
our Lord and our brother.
    Amen.

John 14:2   John 3:16   1 John 4:8, 16.

CARRY THE CROSS EACH DAY

Lord Jesus, you know how earnestly we wish
"instant" joy and happiness, right now,
     without waiting a moment longer.
Yet you tell us:
"Whoever wish to be my followers,
must deny their very selves,
take up their crosses each day,
and follow in my steps."

Grant that we may never be ashamed of these words
     in the presence of our brothers and sisters,
but rather accept them as a rule of life.
For to follow you is to find the cross;
but your cross is a source of joy,
and your joy, during this very day, is the gate to eternity!

FATHER, SOURCE OF ALL JOY

God our Father,
source of all joy in heaven as on earth,
prepare for all people, we pray,
     the banquet of eternal joy.

Remove the mourning veil covering all peoples
and the shroud investing all nations.

Destroy death forever
in the resurrection of your Son Jesus.

Wipe away the tears from every cheek;
take away the shame of the people who love you.

     Because you are God
for the joy and gladness of all people,
you have not created death or invented tears;
but you call all people to be brothers and sisters of Jesus,
to share your life and joy
     forever.

Luke 9:23-26   Isaiah 25:6-8   Wisdom 1:13   1 Corinthians 15:26.

YES, FATHER, FOR THAT IS YOUR GRACIOUS WILL

We thank you, God our Father,
for having taught us to say with your Spirit
   who dwells in our hearts:
"Yes, Father, for that is your gracious will!"

When we say this "yes"
in our joys as well as in our sorrows,
   be so kind as to recognize
the voice of Jesus, your beloved Son!

THE WIDOW OF NAIM

May you be blessed, Lord Jesus,
for the day when you encountered the tears
   of the widow of Naim!

God unchangeable in your eternity,
infinite in your goodness,
you whom no misery of ours can affect,
to whose joy no one can add,
   or from which no one can subtract:
May you be blessed, because in Jesus Christ
you allowed yourself to be moved by the tears
   of a widow.

May you be blessed, because now we know
   the God eternal
   has a human heart.
Let our misery become your misery,
so that your joy may become our joy.

Matthew 11:26 Luke 10:21 Luke 7:11-17.

TWO BROTHERS

For a very long time,
two brothers have been at war with each other
and have made the heart of their father sad.

One is the Jewish people, born of Isaac;
the other, the Arabs, born of Ishmael.
Both are sons of Abraham.

You also, Lord Jesus,
are a son of Abraham.

You who, by your cross, have destroyed hatred
and established the peace of God,
reconcile your brothers according to the flesh,
so that the people born of Abraham
may finally be the people of peace.

And, at the time foreseen according to your mercy,
let them recognize you
for their Savior and their brother.

THE AMEN OF OUR LOVE

Praise and glory to you, Jesus,
our Lord and our brother!

In you "Yes" and "No" were never found
        side by side;
rather for our sakes you were the total "Yes,"
which the love of God pronounced on our behalf,
and in which he kept all his promises.

        We pray to you:
Please be our "Amen" of love that we offer
        in return
        for the love of your Father.

The Amen of Our Love, *2 Corinthians 1:20-22.*

MORNING
PRAYERS

GIVE US, O LORD

Let us ask the Father of lights,
from whom we receive every gift,
to open our hearts to his grace:
    Lord, grant us your love.

Give us, O Lord,
a day filled with your presence
and bright with your love.
    Lord, grant us your love.

Give us, O Lord,
your angel to guide us on our way
and to watch over our souls and bodies.
    Lord, grant us your love.

Give us, O Lord,
your joy in our sadness,
your light in our darkness.
    Lord, grant us your love.

Give us, O Lord,
our daily bread,
and forgive us our sins.
    Lord, grant us your love.

Give us, O Lord,
a life lived in grace,
a death in the peace of your love.
    Lord, grant us your love.

Give us, O Lord,
your mercy on the last day,
and the Kingdom you have prepared for us.
    Lord, grant us your love.

PRAYER OF CONTEMPLATION

In the morning,
I sing your praise, O Lord.

Lord, you have always given me
    tomorrow's bread,
and, although I am poor,
    today I believe.

Lord, you have always mapped out
    tomorrow's road,
and, although it is hidden,
    today I believe.

Lord, you have always given me
    tomorrow's peace,
and, in spite of my distress,
    today I believe.

Lord, you have always given me
    tomorrow's strength,
and, although I am weak,
    today I believe.

Lord, you have always given me
    tomorrow's light,
and, in spite of the darkness,
    today I believe.

Lord, you have always spoken
    when I was in doubt,
and, in spite of your silence,
    today I believe.

Lord, you are my life;
    you are my endless joy.
Even in death
    forever I believe.

PRAYER OF PSALM 146

(In the morning, Ps 90:14)

Fill us with your love in the morning
and we will live the whole day
in joy and praise.
   Lord, listen to us.

(In the evening, Ps 141:2)

Let my prayer rise before you like incense,
and my hands like the evening offering.
   Lord, listen to us.

Restore sight to the blind;
straighten those who are bent.
   Lord, listen to us.

Protect the weak and the needy;
support the widow and the orphan.
   Lord, listen to us.

Come and cure all broken hearts;
give justice to the oppressed.
   Lord, listen to us.

Give bread to the hungry;
give freedom to prisoners.
   Lord, listen to us.

May your eternal Kingdom be ours;
give salvation to those who love you.
   Lord, listen to us.

IF TODAY YOU HEAR HIS VOICE

God of truth, you who said to us,
"If today you hear my voice,
harden not your hearts,"
we pray to you at the beginning of this day.

You who speak to us through the marvels of creation,
which you give us for our joy:
Open our eyes that we may recognize therein
the trace of your steps.

You who speak to us through today's happenings:
Make us attentive so as to discern your holy will
in each of our joys and our pains.

You who speak to us through our brothers and sisters:
Help us to discover your face
in the faces of those who surround us.

You who speak to us through your Son, your living Word,
announced by the prophets
and proclaimed by the Evangelists:

You who speak to us even in your silences:

Give us the grace to open our hearts to your calls,
to listen to them with joy,
to follow them with love,
until the twilight of our lives,
when we will arrive at that eternal today,
when we will see you face to face,
forever and ever.
        Amen!

Psalm 95:7-8.

WAKE OUR SLEEPING HEARTS

Our Father in heaven,
you who lead us from the darkness of night
to the brightness of this new day,
     listen to our prayer.

Let your grace wake our sleeping hearts.

Let our words, our thoughts, and our actions,
today and all the days of our lives,
be always concerned with the accomplishment
     of your holy will.

Preserve us from the sadness of sin;
keep us in the joy of your light.

Then, when evening comes,
we will be able, now and always,
to praise, bless, and glorify you,

through Jesus Christ, your beloved Son,
in the unity of the Holy Spirit,
forever and ever.
     Amen!

MAKE YOUR LIGHT SHINE

God our Father, you who said,
"Let there be light shining out of darkness!"
make your light shine in our hearts
so that the knowledge of the glory of God,
which is on the face of Christ,
may shine brightly there.

Throughout this day,
may your mercy be our defense;
your praise, our gladness;
your Word, the treasure of our hearts.

Let your blessing descend on each of our actions.
Let it accompany us and help us reach
the great morning that knows no night,
when we will praise your love unceasingly,

through your Son, Jesus Christ, our Savior and our brother,
in the unity of the love of the Holy Spirit,
forever and ever.
    Amen!

2 Corinthians 4:6.

TO ASSEMBLE FOR YOUR PRAISE

God our Father, you who, in Jesus Christ,
have called us from darkness into your marvelous light
so that we may announce your praises and your splendor:

We bless you; we adore you;
we glorify you at all times,
but especially on this morning
when you have awakened us to assemble for your praise.

Help us today and every day to love you more
by loving our brothers and sisters with greater sincerity.

When the morning of eternal Day dawns,
grant us a place on your right hand.
Then, with smiles on our lips and joy in our hearts,
we will celebrate the strength of your love,
forever and ever.
      Amen!

OPEN MY EAR

Every morning, Lord,
open my ear
that I may hear your Word.

I am your disciple:
Teach me
in your Son Jesus Christ.

1 Peter 2:9 Isaiah 50:4.

THAT WE MAY LEARN TO LOVE YOU

Blessed are you Lord, our Father,
you who give us this new day
to learn to love you more.

Help us today and every day
to look for you and to find you
in the service of our brothers and sisters.

Illumine the eyes of our hearts
so that, in each of our joys and our sorrows,
we will know how to recognize your presence,
to discover your tenderness,
and to live in your peace.

And just as you lead us
from the shades of night to the brightness of morn,
lead us beyond the darkness and joys of this world
to the light and the joy of the eternal Day.

Yours be our love and our praise,
in the Church and Christ Jesus,
forever and ever.
      Amen!

O RISING SUN!

At the dawning of this new day,
Lord Jesus, we offer you our prayer:

Light of life that shines in the darkness!
Be so kind as to bestow on all people,
        our brothers and sisters,
your splendor and your truth
so that they may recognize you as Savior,
and give them your life and your joy
so that they will love you as God.

Gather up into your Kingdom of light
all who have died during the night —
we commend them to your mercy.

Also console with your divine peace
all who, during the night,
have carried the burden of sickness,
the distress of sadness,
or the bitterness of loneliness.

O Rising Sun! Come to light up
those who still sleep in the darkness of death.

Guide our footsteps on the road of peace
to your Father, who is also our Father,
for you are our way, our truth, and our life,
        forever and ever.
        Amen!

Luke 2:78-79   John 8:12; 14:6.

SHOW US THE LIGHT OF YOUR FACE

When daylight comes,
Lord, we give you thanks,
and we implore you:
Show us the light of your face.

Direct and sanctify, rule and govern
our hearts and our bodies,
our feelings, our words and our deeds,
according to your law of love.

Help us today and every day
to share in building a more beautiful world,
founded on Jesus Christ, in justice and love.

By spreading your joy and peace around us,
by driving back the frontiers of suffering and death,
may we be able to announce by our entire lives
the future Kingdom, where you will dry all tears
    on the Day of eternity.
    Amen!

THE SMILE OF YOUR FACE

Lord, the smile of the dawn
lights up the sky.

May the smile of your face
light up our day!

Psalm 4:7.

MAKE YOUR LOVE RISE ON ALL

God of tenderness and pity,
we pray at the beginning of this day:

Just as you cause your sun to rise
on the good and the wicked,
let your love rise on all people, our brothers and sisters.

All that we are, all that we have,
we put back in your hands
so that this day may be completely consecrated.

We offer all to you through Jesus, your beloved Son,
our Lord and our High Priest,
who sits at your right hand
to intercede without ceasing on our behalf
and to help us to enter the eternal Kingdom,
where we will enjoy the fullness of joy and peace,
forever and ever.
        Amen!

Matthew 5:45 Hebrews 7:25.

EVENING
PRAYERS

STAY WITH US, LORD

Stay with us, Lord Jesus Christ!

Stay with us, Lord:
Behold, evening is coming,
and we still have not recognized your face
in each of our brothers and sisters.
Stay with us, Lord Jesus Christ!

Stay with us, Lord:
Behold, evening is coming,
and we still have not shared your bread
in thanksgiving with all our brothers and sisters.
Stay with us, Lord Jesus Christ!

Stay with us, Lord:
Behold, evening is coming,
and we still have not recognized your Word
in the words of all our brothers and sisters.
Stay with us, Lord Jesus Christ!

Stay with us, Lord:
Behold, evening is coming,
and our hearts are still too slow to believe
that you had to die in order to rise again.
Stay with us, Lord Jesus Christ!

Stay with us, Lord,
for our night itself becomes day
    when you are there!
Stay with us, Lord Jesus Christ!

ALL DAY LONG, LORD

Remember us, O Lord,
in your loving care!

All day long, Lord,
I have waited for you on my doorstep,
and, behold, you were in my house!
　　Remember us, O Lord,
　　in your loving care!

All day long, Lord,
I have looked for you far off in the crowd,
and, behold, you were right next to me,
present in my brother and my sister!
　　Remember us, O Lord,
　　in your loving care!

All day long, Lord,
my hands remained closed
to protect my happiness,
and, behold, my happiness
was to open them for you!
　　Remember us, O Lord,
　　in your loving care!

All day long, Lord,
I looked for your Word
in the wisdom of men and women,
and, behold, it was present
in the depths of my heart!
　　Remember us, O Lord,
　　in your loving care!

I TRUST IN YOU, LORD

*Into your hands, O Lord,
I commend my spirit.*

I trust in you, Lord; deliver me;
    my life is in your hands;
through your love save me.
Into your hands, O Lord, I commend my spirit.

Look at me; answer me, Lord my God;
    open my eyes
that I may not sleep in death.
Into your hands, O Lord, I commend my spirit.

Guard me like the pupil of your eye;
    hide me
in the shadow of your wings.
Into your hands, O Lord, I commend my spirit.

I lie down and sleep in peace;
    you alone, Lord,
keep me safe.
Into your hands, O Lord, I commend my spirit.

In joy I will look upon your face, Lord;
    when I awake
I will be satisfied with your face.
Into your hands, O Lord, I commend my spirit.

Psalms 4:9; 13:4; 17:8, 15; 31:6, 15-17.

I STAND KNOCKING

Lord Jesus, you who said,
"Here I stand, knocking at the door.
If anyone hears me calling and opens the door,
I will enter his house and have supper with him,
and he with me,"
look at your family gathered together before you.

We have heard your living Word;
we open the door of our community to you;
we pray you be our guest.

Let each one of us
in the joys and sorrows of our way
feel the comfort of your presence.

Beyond the darkness of this world,
lead us to the morning of the eternal Day
when you yourself will invite us
to the banquet of the Kingdom
that your Father prepares for us,
forever and ever.
        Amen!

Revelation 3:20.

COME TO ME, ALL YOU WEARY

Lord Jesus, you who said,
"Come to me, all you who are weary
and find life burdensome,
and I will refresh you,"
  we pray to you:

See our hands tired
  from having searched for vanity.
See our spirits wounded
  from having welcomed pride.
See our hearts now aching
  from having loved all except you.

Help us to understand
that carrying your yoke means to rest,
and refusing your burden means to become tired,
for your yoke is easy and your burden light.

Just as you give us this night
  to rest our bodies,
give us your tenderness
  to rest our souls.

By a life rich in good works
  toward our brothers and sisters,
lead us to the kingdom of eternal rest,
where we will experience the fullness of joy and peace
close to our Father, in the love of the Spirit,

forever and ever.
  Amen!

Matthew 11:28-29.

THE EYES OF MARY

Lord Jesus,
have pity on me!

With Martha,
I was busy all day long.

Allow me now,
with Mary,
to sit at your feet
simply to look at you.

THE TIRED HANDS OF MARTHA

Lord Jesus,
I would have chosen, like Mary,
to sit all day long in peace
       at your feet
and listen to the silence of my heart.

But you came into my house
with all your friends
who kept me busy,
and I served them for love of you.

If I cannot offer you
the eyes of Mary,
accept at least, I pray you,
the tired hands of Martha.
They are my love for you.

Luke 10:38-42.

BEYOND THE NIGHT

When evening comes,
Lord, we pray:

We thank you for this day
filled with your presence.

We praise and bless you
for the joy of those who love one another,
for the efforts of those who work,
for the patience of those who suffer,
for every good work that people
have accomplished in your honor today.

We ask pardon of you
for the weakness of our love
on the road that leads to you.

Lead us beyond the night
to the dawn of the eternal Day
when we will see you face to face.

You who are our Father,
your Son Jesus Christ,
who is our Savior and our brother,
and the Holy Spirit who dwells in our hearts,

forever and ever.
    Amen!

LORD JESUS, COME AMONG US

Lord Jesus, who came among us
to call not the virtuous, but the sinners,
it is to you we pray:

With confidence we present ourselves before you,
in spite of our weakness, because you forgive us
not because of our deeds
but according to the abundance of your love.

Gather together your Church,
torn apart by our sins and divisions.
Gather together also our hearts,
scattered by the vanities of this world.

Grant us finally a peaceful evening,
a night of quiet rest,
a morning filled with joy and zeal to serve you.

You are the hope of our lives and our Savior,
forever and ever.
      Amen!

Matthew 9:13.

VISIT OUR COMMUNITY

We ask you, Lord:
Visit our community,
which your love put together.

Remove far from it
every attack of the enemy.

Let your holy angels dwell with us
to keep us in peace.

Let your blessing and your love
come to rest on each one of us.

Save us through your Son Jesus Christ,
who died and rose again for us,
so that, awake or asleep,
we may always live in the joy of your presence,

    forever and ever.
        Amen!

THE CUP OF OUR DAY

When evening comes,
we present to you, Lord,
the cup of our day.

It is empty, you know —
fill it with your pardon.

And our hearts will rest then
in peace and joy.

1 Thessalonians 5:9-10.

WHEN CHRIST, THE MORNING STAR, RISES

We bless you, O God, our Father,
through your only Son, Jesus Christ, the Lord.

Having ended this day,
having arrived at the borders of night,
having been satisfied by the light of the day
that you created for our joy, we thank you
      and ask for your kindness.

Just as you hide all things
in the darkness of night,
please cover our faults
      in your endless mercy.

Be so kind as to send your holy angels
to keep us in peace
and protect us on the roads of our lives.

Gather us into the Kingdom of eternal light
on the day when Christ, the Morning Star,
      rises in our hearts.

We ask this of you through Jesus Christ,
your Son, our Lord,
who lives and reigns with you in the unity
      of the Holy Spirit,
God forever and ever.
      Amen!

2 Peter 1:19.

YOURS ARE THE TIMES OF OUR LIVES

When evening comes,
Lord, we thank you.

Yours is the day; yours is the night;
yours also are the times of our lives:
They are in your hand;
we entrust them to your mercy.

Let the end of this day,
which increases the number of days in our lives,
increase also our love for you.

Forgive us our weaknesses,
you who find joy in showing mercy.

Let nothing hinder us on our way to you.
By our holy lives and our prayers
may we be able to hasten the coming of that day
when you will open the gate of your mercy
to those seeking your love.

To you be glory and power,
through Jesus Christ, your beloved Son,
in the unity of the Holy Spirit,
now and until the day of eternity.
    Amen!

Psalm 74:16   Micah 7:18   2 Peter 3:11-12.

THE BRIDEGROOM IS HERE

Lord Jesus,
see your community assembled before you
for your praise in the evening.

We return to you this day
that your goodness has given us.
Let its joy as well as its dullness
reveal your love to us.

Forgive our weaknesses,
you who are the fullness of mercy.
Take away our fatigue,
you who are the repose of our souls.

Help us to stay awake
and wait joyfully for your return.

When you do return in the middle of the night,
let us be ready to run to you.
When the cry resounds
"The bridegroom is here!"
let us go in with you to the banquet of your Kingdom,

where you reign with your Father,
who is also our Father,
in union with the Spirit of love,
forever and ever.
        Amen!

Matthew 25:6.

A SOURCE OF LIVING WATER

This day has passed away
like water that runs through our fingers.

Lord, we thirst for eternity.
Unearth in our hearts a source of living water
that springs forth unto eternal life.

JOY AND BEAUTY

Lord Jesus, the joy and beauty
of every moment of my life!

Be the last melody of my day song
as it fades into the night.

And tomorrow,
when my eyes greet the morning,
be my first ray of sunlight.

WE BLESS YOU

We bless you, Lord Jesus,
Light born of the Light.

Teach us to flee the darkness of this world
and to hasten toward the day
that the sadness of night
cannot darken.

John 4:14.

GIVE TO MY EYES

Blest be you, Lord Jesus!

Give to my eyes a light sleep
so that my voice, to praise you,
does not remain silent too long.

Your creation will stay awake
so that it may sing with the angels.
May my sleep, in your presence,
be a prayer arising to you.

Let the night retain no faults
    of the past day.
Let not the madness of the night
    invade my dreams.
Even in sleep let my spirit, Lord,
    sing to you.

God, Father and Son and Holy Spirit,
to you be honor, power, and glory,
forever and ever.

St. Gregory Nazianzen (+ 390).

BLESSINGS

Blessed be you, Lord, God of tenderness and compassion,
    rich in kindness and faithfulness,
who keep us in your love forever!   *— Amen.*

The Lord our God is a God of mercy.
To him be glory forever!   *— Amen.*

May the Lord bless us and keep us!   *— Amen.*
May the Lord let his face shine on us
    and be gracious to us!   *— Amen.*
May the Lord show his face to us
    and give us his peace!   *— Amen.*

Blessed be our God from everlasting to everlasting!   *— Amen.*
    And blessed be your name of glory,
which surpasses all blessing and praise!   *— Amen.*

Blessed be God!   *— Amen.*
Blessed be his great name!   *— Amen.*
Blessed be all his holy angels!   *— Amen.*
Blessed be his great name forevermore!   *— Amen.*
Blessed be all his angels forever!   *— Amen.*

Blessed be the Lord, the God of Israel,
    who alone performs marvels!   *— Amen.*
Blessed forever be his glorious name!   *— Amen.*
May the whole world be filled with his glory!   *— Amen.*

    Blessed be you, Lord,
God of the humble and help of the oppressed!   *— Amen.*
    Blessed be you, Lord,
support of the weak and refuge of the forsaken!   *— Amen.*
    Blessed be you, Lord,
savior of the despairing — to you be eternal glory!   *— Amen.*

Blessed be you, Father, Lord of heaven and earth!   *— Amen.*
You hide your mystery from the learned and clever,
but you reveal it to mere children.   *— Amen.*
Yes, Father, for such is your gracious will.   *— Amen.*

Exodus 34:6-7   Deuteronomy 4:31   Numbers 6:24-26   Nehemiah 9:5
Tobias 11:4   Psalm 72:18-19   Judith 9:11   Matthew 11:25-26.

May you be blessed, Lord Jesus,
who died for our sins
and rose again for our life!   —*Amen.*
To you be glory forever!   —*Amen.*

Blessed be the God of hope and consolation!   —*Amen.*
May he help us all to be tolerant with one another,
following the example of Jesus Christ!   —*Amen.*
So that, united in mind and voice, we may give glory
to the God and Father of our Lord Jesus Christ!   —*Amen.*

May the God of hope fill us
with every joy and with peace, in the faith!   —*Amen.*
May hope overflow in us
    through the power of the Holy Spirit!   —*Amen.*

To the Father, who can give us the strength to live
according to the Gospel and the message of Jesus Christ,
to him, the God who alone is wise, through Jesus Christ,
be glory and power forever!   —*Amen.*
May God our Father strengthen us until the last day
      so that we may be without blame
      on the Day of our Lord Jesus Christ!   —*Amen.*
He is faithful, he who calls us
to fellowship with his Son Jesus, our Lord.   —*Amen.*
      To him be glory forever!   —*Amen.*

Let us give thanks to God, who gives us victory
      through our Lord Jesus Christ!   —*Amen.*

Marana tha! Come, Lord Jesus!   —*Amen.*
Your grace be with us all!   —*Amen.*

Blessed be the God and Father
of our Lord Jesus Christ,
a gentle Father and the God of all consolation
who comforts us in all our sorrows!   —*Amen.*

Blessed be God our Father,
who raised his Son Jesus Christ to life!   —*Amen.*
He will raise us one day with him
and place us together by his side.   —*Amen.*

Romans 4:25; 15:5-6; 16:25, 27 1 Corinthians 1:8-9; 15:57; 16:23-24
2 Corinthians 1:3-4; 4:14.

The grace of our Lord Jesus Christ,
the love of God the Father,
and the fellowship of the Holy Spirit
    be with us all!   — *Amen.*

The grace and peace of God our Father
    and the Lord Jesus Christ!   — *Amen.*
He sacrificed himself for our sins
to rescue us from this present wicked world
    in accordance with the will of his Father.   — *Amen.*
To him be glory forever!   — *Amen.*

Blessed be the God and Father
    of our Lord Jesus Christ,
who has filled us with blessings in Christ!   — *Amen.*

Glory to God our Father,
from generation to generation,
in the Church and in Christ Jesus!   — *Amen.*

May God the Father and the Lord Jesus
grant peace, love, and faith to all our brothers and sisters! — *Amen.*
May grace be with all who love
    our Lord Jesus Christ!   — *Amen.*

    May God our Father,
who has begun an excellent work in us,
    see that it is finished
when the Day of Christ Jesus comes!   — *Amen.*
To him be glory forever!   — *Amen.*

May the peace of God that is beyond all understanding
guard our hearts and our thoughts in Christ Jesus!   — *Amen.*

May God our Father fulfill all our needs
according to his generosity, with magnificence,
    in Christ Jesus!   — *Amen.*
To him be glory forever!   — *Amen.*

We give you thanks, our Father!   — *Amen.*
You call us to share the lot of the saints
    in light!   — *Amen.*

2 Corinthians 13:13   Galatians 1:3-5   Ephesians 1:3-4; 3:21; 6:23-24
Philippians 1:6; 4:7; 4:19-20   Colossians 1:12.

You rescue us from the power of darkness
and bring us into the Kingdom
      of your beloved Son.   — *Amen.*

May the peace of God reign in our hearts,
that peace to which we are called together
      as parts of one Body.   — *Amen.*
In all our words and actions
let us give thanks to God our Father,
      in the name of the Lord Jesus.   — *Amen.*

May God our Father put our faith into action,
to work for love, to preserve hope,
      through our Lord Jesus Christ.   — *Amen.*

May the Lord help us to grow and abound
      in love for one another.   — *Amen.*
May he confirm our hearts in holiness without blame
      before God our Father,
at the time of his coming with all his saints.   — *Amen.*

      Blessed be God our Father,
who gives salvation through our Lord Jesus Christ. — *Amen.*
      He died and rose again for us
      so that, awake or asleep,
we might live together with him.   — *Amen.*

      May the Lord of peace himself
give us peace all the time
      and in every way!   — *Amen.*
The Lord be with us all!   — *Amen.*

Grace, mercy, and peace from God our Father
      and Christ Jesus, our Lord!   — *Amen.*

      To the eternal King,
the immortal, invisible, and only God,
be honor and glory forever and ever!   — *Amen.*

To the blessed and only ruler of all,
to the King of kings and Lord of lords,
who alone is immortal,
whose home is unapproachable light,

Colossians 1:13; 3:15-17 1 Thessalonians 1:2; 3:12-13; 5:9-10
2 Thessalonians 3:16 1 Timothy 1:2; 1:17; 6:15.

whom no man has ever seen or can see,
to him be honor and everlasting power!   — *Amen.*

    Jesus Christ, the same
yesterday, today, and forever.   — *Amen.*
To him be glory forever!   — *Amen.*

May God be glorified in all things through Jesus Christ!   — *Amen.*
To him be glory and power forever and ever!   — *Amen.*

May the God of all grace who has called us
to his everlasting glory in Christ Jesus,
    after brief suffering,
restore us to himself and confirm us.   — *Amen.*
May he strengthen us and make us steadfast.   — *Amen.*
To him be power forever and ever!   — *Amen.*

May grace and peace be given us in abundance
    as we come to know God
      and Jesus, our Lord!   — *Amen.*
To him be glory forever and ever!   — *Amen.*

May we grow in the grace and knowledge
of our Lord and Savior, Jesus Christ!   — *Amen.*
To him be glory now and in eternity!   — *Amen.*

To him who can keep you from falling
and bring you safely into his glorious presence,
innocent and happy,
to the only God, our Savior, through Jesus our Lord,
be glory, majesty, authority, and power,
from even before the beginning of time,
through the present,
and for all ages to come.   — *Amen.*

Praise, glory, and wisdom,
thanksgiving, honor, power, and strength,
    to our God
      forever and ever!   — *Amen.*

Amen! Come, Lord Jesus!   — *Amen.*
May your grace be with us all!   — *Amen.*

1 Timothy 6:16   Hebrews 13:8   1 Peter 4:11; 5:10-11   2 Peter 1:2; 3:18
Jude 24-25   Revelation 7:12; 22:21.

RESPONSES

FOR THE

LITANIES

① Al - le - lu - ia, — Al - le - lu - ia, Al - le - lu - ia!

② Blest are those who are in - vit - ed —

— to the ban - quet of the King - dom!

③ Blest are you, O Lord, through e - ter - ni - ty!

Ⓐ Come, Lord Je - sus, come!
or
Ⓑ Come, Lord Je - sus Christ.

⑤ Come, O Lord, come, save your peo - ple!

⑥ Come to pray in us, Spir - it of the Lord!

⑦ Come to us, Spir - it of the Lord!

188

8. De - liv - er us, O Lord!

9. Em - man - u - el! Come, save your peo - ple!

10. Glo - ry and praise to you, Lord Je - sus Christ!

11. Glo - ry to God on high!

12. Grant to us your love.

13. Grant to us your sal - va - tion.

14. Have mer - cy, O Lord, have mer - cy on us!

15. Have mer - cy, O Lord, have mer - cy on us!

16. Hear us, Lord, show us mer - cy!

Help us to fast, O Lord, by lov-ing one an - oth - er.

Ho-ly, ho-ly, ho-ly is the Lord,— for e - ter-nal is his love!

In the morn-ing, I sing your praise, O Lord.

In - to your hands, O Lord, I com-mend my spir-it.

Je - sus Christ, ris - en Lord, have mer - cy on us!

Joy to you, O Vir-gin Mar-y, Moth-er of the Lord!

Lead us not in - to temp - ta - tion,

but de - liv - er us from e - vil!

Let the light of your face shine up-on us!

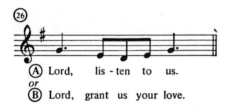

Lord, have mer - cy.

Ⓐ Lord, lis - ten to us.
or
Ⓑ Lord, grant us your love.

Ma - ra - na tha! Come, Lord Je - sus, come!

May you be blest, O Lord!

My Lord and my God!

O God, be mer-ci-ful to me, a sin-ner!

31. O Lord, we pray to you.

32. O-pen my eyes, O Je - sus, Lord.

33. Praise to you, Lord Je - sus Christ, King of end - less glo - ry!

34. Praise to you now and ev - er - more!

35. Praise to you, O Lord!

36. Pray to the Lord for us.

37. Re - mem-ber us, O Lord, in your King - dom.

38. Re - mem-ber us, O Lord, in your lov - ing care.

Save us, O Lord, grant to us your love.

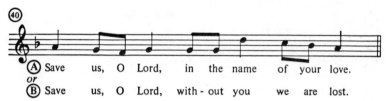

Ⓐ Save us, O Lord, in the name of your love.
or
Ⓑ Save us, O Lord, with-out you we are lost.

Show to us your mer - cy, Lord our God.

Stay with us, Lord Je - sus Christ!

Those trust-ing in you, O Lord, will nev-er be de - ceived.

We sing your praise, O Lord.

You are my love, O Lord, you are my joy!

Your king-dom come, O Lord!

HOLY MOTHER

Holy Mother of our Redeemer,
ever open gate of heaven and star of the sea,
come to the aid of your children
who have fallen and who seek to rise.
You gave birth, O Wonder, to your Creator,
remaining ever virgin.
Receive the greetings of the Angel Gabriel,
and have pity on us sinners.

HAIL, HOLY QUEEN

Hail, holy Queen of the Heavens!
Hail, holy Queen of the Angels!
Hail, Root of Jesse!
Hail, Gate of Heaven!
By you the Light has entered the world.
Rejoice, glorious Virgin,
beautiful among all women.
Hail, radiant Splendor,
intercede with Christ for us.

QUEEN OF HEAVEN

Queen of Heaven, rejoice, Alleluia!
For the Lord whom you were worthy to bear, Alleluia!
Has risen as he said, Alleluia!
Pray for us to God, Alleluia!

WE PLACE OURSELVES

We place ourselves in your keeping,
    holy Mother of God.
Do not refuse the prayer of your children
    in their distress.
But deliver us from all danger,
Ever Virgin, glorious and blessed!

For the musical settings of these texts, see Deiss, *Biblical Hymns and Psalms,*
Vol. I.

TITLE INDEX

ADDITIONAL COPYRIGHT NOTICES